THE COMMONWEALTH ASSOCIATION OF TAX ADMINISTRATORS

Implementing Large Taxpayer Units

The Commonwealth Association of Tax Administrators
Commonwealth Secretariat
Marlborough House, Pall Mall
London SW1Y 5HX
United Kingdom

Designed and produced by the Commonwealth Secretariat.

Printed by Hobbs the Printers Ltd, Totton, Hampshire.

ISBN: 0-9553540-0-5 (10-digit version)
        978-0-9553540-0-7 (13-digit version)

Price: £10.00

Contents

Foreword

Amongst various popular trends in modern tax administrations, that of setting up specialised wings, units or departments for dealing with cases of large taxpayers is one that is attracting a lot of attention in most CATA member countries. Several countries which have very recently embarked upon such projects or are in the planning phase expressed their desire for guidance and best practices material on the subject from CATA. In response, CATA secretariat started this publication aimed at putting together the experience of selected tax administrations that have successfully created specialised departments for exclusive dealing with large taxpayers in their respective countries. The objective of this publication is to highlight the initial planning processes involved, objectives determined and implementation phases systematically delivered in the creation of large taxpayers units. In a nutshell, this is meant to identify the common denominators in success stories. While this publication is primarily meant to assist countries in avoiding pitfalls and short listing recommended steps and measures at the start of the process, it is also likely that the compiled information will be helpful in identifying areas for improvements or taking timely corrective measures by those countries that have already set up such units.

I would like to record my deep appreciation for the hard work put in by Ms Kristy Dam, Deputy Director, Training & Research at CATA in collecting information and compiling this publication. At the same time, CATA would like to record its gratitude and appreciation to those member countries that have contributed time, resource and information on their respective experiences for the collective benefit of all members of CATA.

Zahir Kaleem
Executive Director

Overview of this Publication

Purpose and scope

This publication discusses the establishment of large taxpayer units (LTUs) by CATA[1] member countries. Whilst it provides **a review of the position and status of CATA member countries in relation to LTUs**, the main focus of the publication is on providing **advice and guidance to readers on how to set up a LTU**, based on the experiences of revenue authorities that have implemented one.

The publication is based on two phases of research. Phase 1 involved a quantitative survey issued to CATA member countries and aimed to identify:

- How many member countries had implemented a LTU

- Their main reasons for implementing a LTU

- How they defined a large taxpayer and how many large taxpayers were managed by the LTU

- The main functions of the LTU, including the types of taxes administered

- The structure of the LTU

- Supervision/reporting lines of the LTU

- The nature of staffing arrangements in the LTU

- How they measured the performance of the LTU

- What benefits they have realised from establishing a LTU.

Phase 2 utilised a case analysis approach of the following member countries: Pakistan, South Africa, Sri Lanka, Tanzania, Uganda and Zambia, to identify how they went about setting up their LTU. This included identifying:

- Whether they had to submit a business case for setting up a LTU and the main arguments used in this business case

- What their implementation plan looked like and what were the critical components of this plan

- What legal or special provisions were made (if any) to give power to the LTU

- What computer systems (if any) were introduced

---

[1] Commonwealth Association of Tax Administrators (www.cata-tax.org).

- How they determined resourcing requirements and budgets

- How they dealt with training and staffing issues

- How they managed the balance between focusing on large taxpayers and other taxpayer segments

- The challenges and risks they faced during implementation and how they were overcome

- What factors ensured the success of the LTU.

What is out of scope?

This publication focuses primarily on implementation issues and does not provide a detailed discussion of the benefits of and reasons for setting up large taxpayer units, nor does it provide a detailed review of the performance of LTUs, as both of these issues have already been extensively covered by previous IMF research: see Baer, K. (2002). 'Improving large taxpayers' compliance: A review of country experience', Occasional Paper 215, International Monetary Fund, Washington DC.

Layout of the publication

This publication is divided into the following sections:

Introduction: Provides a brief introduction to the benefits and risks associated with implementing an LTU and some background as to why this publication was developed.

Snap-shot of the position and status of CATA member countries in relation to large taxpayer units: Provides a snap-shot review of the position of CATA member countries in relation to LTUs.

In-depth case studies: Describes the establishment of LTUs in the following case study countries: Pakistan, South Africa, Sri Lanka, Tanzania, Uganda, UK and Zambia.

Common themes and good practices: Summarises the common themes and best practices arising from the case studies and the existing literature.

Feedback

Any feedback about this report can be emailed to the CATA Secretariat at: cata@commonwealth.int.

Limitations

A tax administration's best practices work in the context of its business processes and systems; culture; political, economic and legislative environment; and people. Plucking a best practice and trying to graft it directly onto another organisation, without careful consideration of these factors, is likely to produce unpredictable results. As such, readers are asked to exercise care before implementing any strategies and initiatives discussed in this publication.

The quantitative survey conducted (see Section 5.2 for further information) also does not cover the entire CATA membership.

Acknowledgements

The author would like to thank all CATA members who participated in the quantitative survey, namely:

Greg Farr (Australia); Sabina Walcott-Denny (Barbados); Segolo Lekau (Botswana); Francis Fiekfu (Cameroon); Jack Ranguma (Kenya); Zainol Abidin Rashid (Malaysia); Carmel Conti (Malta); Spyros Papageorgiou (New Zealand); Ifueko Omoigui (Nigeria); Salman Nabi (Pakistan); Betty Palaso (Papua New Guinea); Tiong Heng Chia (Singapore); Mbongeni Manqele (South Africa); Mahinda Medagoda (Sri Lanka); Karen Hobson (St Kitts & Nevis); James Charles (St Lucia); Harry Kitillya (Tanzania); Rajram Basdeo (Trinidad & Tobago); Jacqueline Kobusingye (Uganda); John Powell and John McGinley (United Kingdom); and Mohamed Ismail (Zanzibar).

The author is especially indebted to the following CATA members who provided additional information for the in-depth case studies:

Pakistan Central Board of Revenue: Ashfaq Muhammed

South African Revenue Service: Edward Chr Kieswetter, Aidan Keanly, André Botes, Franz Tomasek, Ahmed Jooma and Lincoln Marais

Sri Lanka Department of Inland Revenue: Mahinda Medagoda

Tanzania Revenue Authority: Harry Kitillya and Patrick Kassera

Uganda Revenue Authority: Jacqueline Kobusingye

UK Her Majesty's Revenue & Customs: John Hudson

Zambia Revenue Authority: Berlin Msiska, Wisdom Nhekairo, Muyangwa Muyangwa, Danmoore Mulima, Kabaye Mwale

The author would also like to acknowledge Zahir Kaleem (Executive Director, CATA), Greg Farr (Second Commissioner Farr, Australian Taxation Office) and Pam Mitchell (Executive Advisor to Second Commissioner Farr, Australian Taxation Office) for their ongoing support and encouragement.

INTRODUCTION

Why this publication was developed

Over the past decade or so, there has been a growing tendency for tax administrations around the world to segment their taxpayer/client base to improve the tailoring and effectiveness of tax compliance programs and taxpayer services. This has been based on the rationale that various segments require different strategies to manage their tax compliance and also because these distinct segments present different revenue risks and service opportunities.

Large taxpayers[2] in particular need tailored strategies to manage the complexity and risks associated with their tax affairs. Large taxpayers have complex business operations, with many operating on a global scale. They have high transaction volumes; act as withholding agents for the taxes of other taxpayers; are often branches of foreign enterprises or own branches themselves; and they employ highly qualified accountants and lawyers. They are also quite a demanding bunch! According to surveys conducted by the UK and Australia[3], the majority of large taxpayers want a relationship of mutual trust with the revenue authority; they want their revenue contacts to have an understanding of their business, including any specific concerns and pressures, and to have an appreciation of their commercial drivers; they want certainty on the tax treatment of transactions as quickly as possible (and preferably in real time); and they want the revenue authority to have transparent processes which enable businesses to predict with reasonable confidence what the revenue authority's attitude to an issue will be.

Research conducted by the IMF in 2002[4] has indeed confirmed that revenue authorities may gain significant benefits from setting up special operations, such as large taxpayer units[5], to manage the compliance of large taxpayers and improve the level of service provided to them. These benefits include:

---

[2] That is, taxpayers that make significant payments and that account for a large percent (50% or more) of total tax collection.

[3] See for example: UK Inland Revenue (2001). 'Review of links with business' (available at: http://www.hmrc.gov.uk/pbr2001/businesslinks.pdf) and Burges, K. (2005). 'Report on the concerns of a number of the largest companies in the large business segment, with ATO audit, investigation, and advice procedures' (available at: http://www.ato.gov.au/large/content.asp?doc=/content/64790.htm).

[4] See Baer, K. (2002). 'Improving large taxpayers' compliance: A review of country experience', Occasional Paper 215, International Monetary Fund, Washington DC.

[5] Also referred to as large taxpayer offices, large taxpayer departments and other similar terms.

- Improved identification, risk assessment and understanding of large taxpayers and their operations

- More timely and accurate return filing and payment by large taxpayers

- Earlier detection of large taxpayers' non-compliance with filing and payment obligations

- More effective audits targeted by economic sector and performed by better-trained inspectors/auditors

- A reduced stock of arrears and therefore more targeted efforts by collection enforcement officers

- Better-trained staff able to deal with more complex tax issues, providing higher quality services to large taxpayers and detecting irregularities and corrupt practices

- Closer scrutiny and supervision of audit staff improving the chances that irregularities and corrupt practices are detected and dealt with.

Other more indirect benefits of establishing LTUs include:

- The introduction of modern systems and procedures to tax administrations as often these new systems and procedures are piloted or introduced in the LTU and then extended to the rest of the organisation. For example, it has been quite common for revenue authorities to pilot a more integrated approach to administering the different tax types in the LTU

- Improved taxpayer perceptions of the tax administration by signalling the government's commitment to enforcing the tax laws – Given the high profile of large taxpayers to the general taxpayer community, it is important for the revenue authority to be perceived as adequately equipped to match the resources of these large taxpayers

- Improved services for large taxpayers, facilitating increased voluntary compliance

- Improved detection and management of the growing problem of tax avoidance as a result of the better policing of that sector of the taxpaying population most likely to indulge in it.

Although LTUs around the world differ in structure, staffing and functions, it is fair to say that most can be placed somewhere along a continuum, ranging from those with a pure compliance focus (more common in developing countries), where the primary goal is closer monitoring of the compliance of large taxpayers, to those with a co-operative compliance focus (more common to transition and developed countries), where the primary goal is to establish closer ties and co-operative relationships[6] with large taxpayers. Where a LTU is placed along this continuum depends very much on the characteristics of the large taxpayer population, the prevailing tax culture and the amount of resources available to the organisation.

But despite the demonstrated benefits of LTUs, IMF research and experience has also identified certain risks associated with setting up LTUs. These include:

- Lack of or weak political support for LTU operations

- Lack of appropriate financial and staff resources

- Failure to grant full responsibility to the LTU for the major tax administration functions

- Sustaining efforts in the long term

- Absence of staff training in specialised areas

- Attracting and retaining staff of sufficiently high calibre to deal with large taxpayers who often have access to the best tax advisors and resources

- Assigning too few or too many taxpayers to the LTU

- Overemphasising the administration of the large taxpayers and ignoring the medium-size and small taxpayers

- Resistance from the local offices to the LTU and the transfer of large taxpayers to the LTU

- Facilitating irregular or corrupt practices by LTU officials who are not properly supervised.

Without careful consideration and addressing of these risks, an LTU is unlikely to deliver on expectations and will achieve sub-optimal performance in the long run. Therefore, a publication which identifies and draws together the lessons and best practices identified amongst the CATA community on how to set up a LTU, will be a valuable reference for member countries that are thinking of implementing or are in the process of implementing a LTU.

---

[6] Those interested in 'co-operative compliance' approaches adopted by some revenue agencies can visit the following web pages: Australian Taxation Office: http://www.ato.gov.au/large/content.asp?doc=/content/22630.htm; Irish Tax and Customs: http://www.revenue.ie/services/bus_large_business.htm; Canada Revenue Agency: http://www.cra-arc.gc.ca/tax/nonresidents/comp/apa-e.html.

Methodology

A two-phased research methodology was used:

Phase 1 – A quantitative survey of CATA member countries was conducted to identify their position and status in relation to the establishment of LTUs. The questionnaire was based on the IMF questionnaire[7] to allow some general comparisons to be made and was distributed to delegates at the Twenty-sixth CATA Annual Technical Conference/Workshop held in Ottawa, Canada from the 28th August – 2nd September 2005. A total of 21 responses were received by mid October 2005, representing approximately 46% of the CATA membership (please see Appendix A for a list of countries that participated in the survey). This represents a range of developing, transition and developed countries with a vast geographical spread.

Phase 2 – Following the quantitative survey, case analysis of the following CATA member countries was carried out: Pakistan, South Africa, Sri Lanka, Tanzania, Uganda, UK and Zambia, to identify how they went about setting up their LTU, including the challenges faced and success factors. For South Africa, Tanzania and Zambia, face-to-face interviews were conducted with relevant LTU staff. For Pakistan, Sri Lanka and Uganda, a self-completion questionnaire was sent to the relevant contacts. For the UK, material delivered at the 2005 CATA CTIC and AMP courses was used, as well as information from HMRC's website (www.hmrc.gov.uk). Phase 2 was carried out during October 2005 – January 2006.

This publication also draws on research studies conducted by others, such as the IMF. In particular, readers are encouraged to refer to the comprehensive IMF publication: Baer, K. (2002). 'Improving large taxpayers' compliance: A review of country experience', Occasional Paper 215, International Monetary Fund, Washington DC. It analyses the organisation, systems and procedures used by 40 countries to monitor the compliance of large taxpayers. It also provides readers with some key lessons in establishing LTUs and describes certain minium requirements an LTU must meet to be fully effective.

Other useful references include:

McCarten, W. (2004). 'Focusing on the few: The role of large taxpayer units in the revenue strategies of developing countries' *(draft paper)*, World Bank, South Asia Region. Available at: http://isp-aysps.gsu.edu/academics/conferences/conf2004/McCarten.pdf.

---

[7] From Baer, K. (2002). 'Improving large taxpayers' compliance: A review of country experience', Occasional Paper 215, International Monetary Fund, Washington DC.

Shome, P. (2004). 'Tax administration and the small taxpayer', Policy Discussion Paper PDP/04/2, International Monetary Fund.
Available at: http://www.imf.org/external/pubs/ft/pdp/2004/pdp02.pdf.

HM Treasury and Inland Revenue (2001). 'Large business taxation: The government's strategy and corporate tax reforms – A consultation document'.
Available at: http://archive.treasury.gov.uk/pdf/2001/large_bus_tax.pdf.

UK Inland Revenue (2001). 'Review of links with business'.
Available at: http://www.hmrc.gov.uk/pbr2001/businesslinks.pdf.

Australian Taxation Office (2000). 'Co-operative compliance: Working with large business in the new tax system'.
Available at: http://www.ato.gov.au/large/content.asp?doc=/content/22630.htm&mnu=27525&mfp=001/009.

Forum on Tax Administration Compliance Sub-group (2004). 'Guidance note – Compliance risk management: Managing and improving tax compliance', OECD Centre for Tax Policy and Administration.
Available at: http://www.oecd.org/dataoecd/44/19/33818656.pdf.

Deloitte (2005). 'Final report: Review of the GST large corporate compliance program' (prepared for the Australian Taxation Office).
Available at: http://ato.gov.au/content/downloads/GSTLCCPFinalReport.pdf.

SNAP-SHOT OF THE POSITION AND STATUS OF CATA MEMBER COUNTRIES IN RELATION TO LARGE TAXPAYER UNITS

Table 1. LTUs in the CATA Community – Summary of key features

Country	Have implemented a LTU	Year of imple-mentation	Criteria used to select large taxpayers	Approx. number of large taxpayers managed/ As percentage of total taxpayers/ As percentage of revenue collection	LTU functions	Taxes administered by the LTU	Approx. number of LTU staff/ As percentage of all staff	Approx. distribution of LTU staff
Australia	Yes	1994	Annual turnover above 100 million AUD (approx. 74 million USD) and value of assets above 30 million AUD (approx. 22 million USD) for high wealth individuals (Note: all members of a corporate group are treated as one group)	1800 business groups and 800 high wealth individuals <1% 34%	Audit Taxpayer services Limited collections monitoring Advice Treaty negotiation	VAT/GST/sales tax Excises and other indirect taxes Personal income tax Corporate income tax Superannuation	2235 10%	50% in audit 50% in taxpayer services/ education

Country	Have implemented a LTU	Year of imple- mentation	Criteria used to select large taxpayers	Approx. number of large taxpayers managed/ As percentage of total taxpayers/ As percentage of revenue collection	LTU functions	Taxes administered by the LTU	Approx. number of LTU staff/ As percentage of all staff	Approx. distribution of LTU staff
Barbados	No – but plan to	-	-	-	-	-	-	-
Botswana	No – but plan to	-	-	-	-	-	-	-
Cameroon	Yes	2004	Amount of taxes paid during previous year/ filing period Annual turnover (Note: all members of a corporate group are treated as one group)	500 NA[8] 80%	Filing and payment Audit Collection enforcement Taxpayer services	VAT/GST/sales tax Excises and other indirect taxes Personal income tax Corporate income tax Local taxes Forestry taxes Petroleum taxes Mining taxes	94 5%	31% in processing and accounting for tax returns and payments 31% in audit 19% in collection enforcement 3% in taxpayer services/ education 5% in computer and statistics 9% in personnel

[8] NA = Not available.

Country	Have implemented a LTU	Year of imple- mentation	Criteria used to select large taxpayers	Approx. number of large taxpayers managed/ As percentage of total taxpayers/ As percentage of revenue collection	LTU functions	Taxes administered by the LTU	Approx. number of LTU staff/ As percentage of all staff	Approx. distribution of LTU staff
Kenya	Yes	1995	Annual turnover Taxpayer is a public enterprise/ financial sector enterprise Specialised industries e.g. insurance, banks, oil, construction Top 200 VAT payers Top 30 Excise Duty payers	580 10% 60%	Audit Collection enforce- ment Taxpayer services	VAT/GST/sales tax Excises and other indirect taxes Personal income tax	120 10% of Domestic Tax Department 4% of KRA	70% in audit 20% in collection enforcement 10% in taxpayer services/ education
Malaysia	Yes	1980s	Amount of taxes paid during previous year/ filing period Annual turnover	NA 10%	Audit Taxpayer services	Corporate income tax Personal income tax Corporate income tax	NA NA	90% in audit 10% in taxpayer services/ education
Malta	No	-	-	-	-	-	-	-

Country	Have implemented a LTU	Year of implementation	Criteria used to select large taxpayers	Approx. number of large taxpayers managed/ As percentage of total taxpayers/ As percentage of revenue collection	LTU functions	Taxes administered by the LTU	Approx. number of LTU staff/ As percentage of all staff	Approx. distribution of LTU staff
New Zealand	Yes	1994	Annual turnover Taxpayer is a public enterprise/ financial sector enterprise Specialist industries irrelevant of turnover	4500 0.02% 55%	Filing and payment Audit Collection enforce- ment Taxpayer services Updating registration Advice	VAT/GST/sales tax Corporate income tax PAYE	280 6%	60% in audit (including risk and intelligence) 3% in collection enforcement 24% in taxpayer services/ education 13% in management, monitoring, reporting and administration

Country	Have implemented a LTU	Year of implementation	Criteria used to select large taxpayers	Approx. number of large taxpayers managed/ As percentage of total taxpayers/ As percentage of revenue collection	LTU functions	Taxes administered by the LTU	Approx. number of LTU staff/ As percentage of all staff	Approx. distribution of LTU staff
Nigeria	Yes	2003	Annual turnover Taxpayer is a public enterprise/ financial sector enterprise Industry sector e.g. oil and gas	Have a large taxpayers department with five large tax offices – each handling 500 taxpayers 1% 90%	Filing and payment Collection enforcement Taxpayer services Updating registration	VAT/GST/sales tax Personal income tax Corporate income tax	500 6.5%	40% in processing and accounting for tax returns and payments 40% in collection enforcement 10% in taxpayer services/ education 10% in information systems (Have a separate audit function independent of tax office)

Country	Have implemented a LTU	Year of implementation	Criteria used to select large taxpayers	Approx. number of large taxpayers managed/ As percentage of total taxpayers/ As percentage of revenue collection	LTU functions	Taxes administered by the LTU	Approx. number of LTU staff/ As percentage of all staff	Approx. distribution of LTU staff
Pakistan	Yes	2002 (Karachi) 2004 (Lahore)	Amount of taxes paid during previous year/filing period Annual turnover Banks and insurance companies Non-resident corporate taxpayers	600 (Karachi only) NA 20%	"One-stop-shop" Filing and payment Audit Collection enforcement Taxpayer services Defence of cases	VAT/GST/sales tax Excises and other indirect taxes Personal income tax Corporate income tax	140 <1%	20% in processing and accounting for tax returns and payments 30% in audit 40% in collection enforcement 5% in taxpayer services/ education 5% in information systems
Papua New Guinea	No – but plan to	-	-	-	-	-	-	-

Country	Have implemented a LTU	Year of implementation	Criteria used to select large taxpayers	Approx. number of large taxpayers managed / As percentage of total taxpayers / As percentage of revenue collection	LTU functions	Taxes administered by the LTU	Approx. number of LTU staff / As percentage of all staff	Approx. distribution of LTU staff
Singapore	Yes	Corporate tax: mid eighties GST: 2004	Annual turnover Taxpayer is a public enterprise/financial sector enterprise For corporate tax: specialised industries such as oil industry, real estate property sector companies, MNCs and companies awarded with tax incentives and amount of investments exceeds certain threshold. For GST: LTU is firstly by tax type and within GST, the criterion that is used to define large taxpayer is by nature of industry. So far, taxpayers in the following industries are classified GST-LTU – Finance, Manufacturing & Logistics, Telecos, Real Estate and Construction.	Corporate tax: 6000 5% 75% GST: 21000 10% 70-80%	Audit Taxpayer services Updating registration Conduct detailed examination of returns and accounts and finalisation of tax assessments Conduct issue-based field visits Handle taxpayers' enquiries and taxpayer education Handle requests for advance rulings Do research and	VAT/ GST/ sales tax Corporate income tax	Corporate tax: 47 3% GST: 40 2.5%	Corporate tax: Each LTU officer is allocated with a portfolio of taxpayers and is responsible for the main functions described. The payment, collection enforcement and information systems are handled by the Payment & Enforcement & IT Divisions GST: 68% in audit 22% in taxpayer services/ education 10% in research, rule review, ruling

Country	Have implemented a LTU	Year of implementation	Criteria used to select large taxpayers	Approx. number of large taxpayers managed/ As percentage of total taxpayers/ As percentage of revenue collection	LTU functions	Taxes administered by the LTU	Approx. number of LTU staff/ As percentage of all staff	Approx. distribution of LTU staff
South Africa	Yes	2004	Companies listed on the JSE Securities Exchange Unlisted companies and groups of companies with an annual turnover greater than 250 million ZAR (approx. 40 million USD) Parastatals (large state owned enterprises) Major financial institutions International enterprises and their local branches	16000 NA 70-80%	"One-stop-shop" Filing and payment Audit Collection enforcement Taxpayer services Updating registration Customs Risk profiling Criminal investigations Dispute resolution Public rulings Advance pricing agreements	VAT/GST/sales tax Personal income tax Corporate income tax PAYE Unemployment insurance Skills development levy Uncertified insurance tax Donations tax Royalties tax Stamp duties Customs	350 (currently)	NA

Country	Have implemented a LTU	Year of implementation	Criteria used to select large taxpayers	Approx. number of large taxpayers managed/ As percentage of total taxpayers/ As percentage of revenue collection	LTU functions	Taxes administered by the LTU	Approx. number of LTU staff/ As percentage of all staff	Approx. distribution of LTU staff
Sri Lanka	Yes	1996	Amount of taxes paid during previous year/filing period; Annual turnover; Number of employees; Level of imports/exports	1000; 6% (corporate taxpayers only); 30%	"One-stop-shop"; Filing & payment; Audit; Collection enforcement; Taxpayer services; Updating registration	VAT/GST/sales tax; Corporate income tax; PAYE	100; 8%	96% in audit and collection enforcement; 2% in processing and accounting for tax returns and payments; 2% in taxpayer services/education
St Kitts & Nevis	No	-	-	-	-	-	-	-
St Lucia	No – but plan to	-	-	-	-	-	-	-

Country	Have implemented a LTU	Year of implementation	Criteria used to select large taxpayers	Approx. number of large taxpayers managed/ As percentage of total taxpayers/ As percentage of revenue collection	LTU functions	Taxes administered by the LTU	Approx. number of LTU staff/ As percentage of all staff	Approx. distribution of LTU staff
United Republic of Tanzania	Yes	2001	Total turnover exceeding 10 billion TSH (approx. 10 million USD) Aggregate tax payment exceeding 400 million TSH (approx. 400000 USD) for three consecutive years Specific sector or trade industries such as financial institutions, oil marketing companies and large mining companies	300 <10% 70% of domestic revenue 30% of all revenue	"One-stop-shop" Filing & payment Audit Collection enforcement Taxpayer services	VAT/GST/sales tax Excises and other indirect taxes Corporate income tax PAYE	85 <3%	42% in audit Remainder split across operational, taxpayer services/ education, technical/law, IT and HR

Country	Have implemented a LTU	Year of implementation	Criteria used to select large taxpayers	Approx. number of large taxpayers managed/ As percentage of total taxpayers/ As percentage of revenue collection	LTU functions	Taxes administered by the LTU	Approx. number of LTU staff/ As percentage of all staff	Approx. distribution of LTU staff
Trinidad and Tobago	Yes	2004	Annual turnover	100 10% 60%	Filing & payment Audit Taxpayer services Updating registration	VAT/GST/sales tax Personal income tax Corporate income tax	100 33% of all auditors 10% of total staff	All staff involved in audit, taxpayer services/ education
Uganda	Yes	1998 (re-launched in 2005)	Amount of taxes paid during previous year/ filing period Annual turnover Number of employees Taxpayer is a public enterprise/ financial sector enterprise Excisable firms (Note: all members of a corporate group are treated as one group)	480 <15% 70%	"One-stop-shop" Filing & payment Audit Collection enforce-ment Taxpayer services	VAT/GST/sales tax Excises and other indirect taxes Corporate income tax Local taxes	100 7%	30% in processing and accounting for tax returns and payments 40% in audit 15% collection enforcement 5% taxpayer services/ education 10% information systems

Country	Have implemented a LTU	Year of implementation	Criteria used to select large taxpayers	Approx. number of large taxpayers managed/ As percentage of total taxpayers/ As percentage of revenue collection	LTU functions	Taxes administered by the LTU	Approx. number of LTU staff/ As percentage of all staff	Approx. distribution of LTU staff
United Kingdom	Yes	Previous Large Business Office: 1997

New Large Business Service: 2005 | Amount of taxes paid during previous year/filing period

Level of imports/exports

VAT throughput in excess of 100 million GBP (175 million USD)

VAT yield in excess of 12 million GBP (21 million USD)

High risk traders

Excise and customs duty throughput in excess of 10 million GBP (17 million USD)

Combined revenue of all taxes in excess of 20 million GBP (35 million USD)

Strategically important business

Scoring system based on size of business, compliance history, behavioural and structural factors | 2195
<1%
NA | Tax compliance work

Audit

Customer service

Support | VAT/GST/ sales tax

Excises and other indirect taxes

Personal income tax

Corporate income tax

Customs duties

National Insurance Contributions | 1987
1.6% | 80% in audit and compliance

10% in customer education

10% in support services |
| Zanzibar | No – but plan to | - | - | - | - | - | - | - |

18

Basic characteristics of large taxpayer units in the CATA community

How many CATA countries have implemented a LTU?

Two thirds of CATA countries surveyed (14 out of 21 countries) had implemented a LTU. Of the seven that had not implemented a LTU, five had plans to implement a LTU in the near future, whilst the two remaining countries did not really see a need for a LTU given the relatively small population of large taxpayers in their country.

Criteria used to select large taxpayers

The criteria used for selecting large taxpayers varied from country to country, although using 'annual turnover' was the most common criterion, adopted by 79% of those with a LTU. Other common criteria used included the 'amount of taxes paid during previous year/filing periods' (50%), 'the taxpayer is a public enterprise or financial sector enterprise' (43%) and 'particular high risk or complex industries or sectors' (often regardless of turnover) (43%).

The IMF points out that there are problems around using the amount of tax paid historically as the <u>only</u> basis for selecting large taxpayers because the following groups of taxpayers could be excluded:

Taxpayers who regularly underreport or underpay tax

Large firms enjoying tax holiday

Large exporters with significant amounts of refunds.

It is thus good to see that all countries which had adopted this criterion have combined it with others to select their large taxpayers.

Number of large taxpayers managed by the LTU

The number of large taxpayers managed by the LTUs varied widely from country to country (ranging from 100 clients to several thousand clients) depending on both the resources and capacity of the administration and the primary responsibilities and functions of the LTU. But as a proportion of the total number of taxpayers managed and the proportion of total revenue collected, for most tax administrations surveyed, large taxpayers represented approximately 1%-15% of the total number of taxpayers managed and 50-80% of revenue collected.

Main functions of the LTU

For the majority of those surveyed, the main functions of the LTU were taxpayer services (which includes providing advice, rulings and advance pricing arrangements in some cases) (93%), audit (86%) and collection enforcement (57%). Other functions included filing and payment (50%) and updating registration (43%). The natural prevalence of international issues amongst large taxpayers has also meant that a few LTUs partake in negotiating and updating tax treaties. A couple of revenue authorities have truly adopted the one-stop-shop concept and handle court cases and related proceedings as well. For example, the South African Revenue Service has even established a Tax Court at their Large Business Centre.

Types of taxes administered by the LTU

In terms of the types of taxes administered by the LTUs, most were responsible for corporate income tax (93%), VAT/GST/sales tax (86%), and personal income tax (57%). Some also administered excises and other indirect taxes (43%) and PAYE (21%). Only two members surveyed indicated that their LTU administered local taxes.

Main reasons for establishing a LTU

Consistent with the IMF findings, the main reasons for establishing a LTU were to provide better services to large taxpayers (100%), to secure revenue/enhance compliance (86%) and to improve the audit program (57%). Other reasons included improving debt collection (50%), improving the management of arrears (43%) and trialling new systems and procedures (36%). Nigeria also commented that the setting up of their LTU has concurrently allowed them to focus better on other taxpayer groups as well.

LTU structure and organisation

Forty three percent of countries surveyed had a single LTU, whilst 43% had a single LTU with branch offices[9]. The remaining 14% had multiple autonomous LTUs.

Not surprisingly, those with a single LTU tended to have supervision/reporting lines where the LTU reported directly to the head of the tax administration, whilst those with a single LTU and branch offices typically had a special headquarters unit in charge of supervising LTU operations.

The majority of LTUs are organised along functional lines or a combination of function and tax type. However, a newer trend emerging is to base the organisation of the LTU on particular industries or sectors. The UK is an interesting case because the recent merger of the former Inland Revenue and Customs & Excise Departments has prompted the need to rationalise and merge the functions of the previous large business units. Currently, the LTU is organised by industry sectors

[9] Although in the case of Kenya, there are no branch offices per se but regional relationship managers.

for indirect taxes and tax category for direct taxes. But from April 2006, the LTU will be organised entirely by industry sectors with single point of contact in HMRC (see Section 7.6 for further detail). Similarly, New Zealand and South Africa have organised their LTUs on the basis of industry sectors.

In terms of staff numbers, LTUs typically employ about 1-12% of the total number of revenue staff, again depending on the responsibilities and functions of the LTU, as well as the available finances and resources. There is however, no clear pattern in terms of the division of staff amongst the various work types, apart from the higher assignment of staff to audit (ranging from 20-100%) compared to other duties such as taxpayer services, processing and collection enforcement (which typically ranges from 0-50%). It is also important to point out that in some of the smaller LTUs, staff commonly perform multiple roles. Many revenue authorities have centralised, corporate-wide functions as well, such as bulk processing, taxpayer services and investigations and prosecutions, to support the activities of the LTU and other business areas or departments.

Performance of LTUs

Performance indicators used

The most commonly used performance indicators to gauge the success of the LTU included 'revenue collected against targets', 'audit coverage' and 'reduction in debt'. Other less commonly used indicators included:

- Adherence to customer service standards (such as time to finalise audits and assessments, effect refunds or respond to taxpayer queries)
- Filing and payment ratios
- Number of cases settled
- Number of objections per assessment raised
- Cost of collection
- Number of new taxpayer registrations
- A total quality management approach to individual case handling, where the quality measures are independently audited and include adherence to propriety procedures.

A few revenue administrations are introducing softer measures to gauge the success of the LTU, such as taxpayer perceptions of the quality of service delivered.

Assessment of the effectiveness of LTUs

Congruent with earlier IMF findings, all revenue authorities surveyed commented positively on the effectiveness of their LTU. The comments provided revolved around the ability of the LTU to increase compliance and revenue via:

- More focused and better quality assessments, investigations and audits done by better qualified staff

- Effective monitoring and follow-up of large taxpayers

- Better provision of customer service, including timely and tailored advice and coordinated interventions, which has the related effect of reducing the compliance burden

- Improved ability in risk identification, especially in areas of tax avoidance.

Closer relationships with large taxpayers have also led to an improved understanding of their business and operating environment and has allowed for earlier identification of risks and issues and a more collaborative approach to ensuring tax compliance. A few others also commented on the rewarding nature of the work for LTU staff, particularly where better pay and incentives have been introduced. For Pakistan, the closer monitoring of tax collectors, both in their work and in their contacts with taxpayers, has helped to better control corruption.

Some of the comments provided by CATA members on the performance of their LTU included the following:

Kenya

"More resources are being added for desired effectiveness but establishing a LTU is certainly the way to go to achieve results with minimum resources".

Tanzania

"The LTU has been very effective in audits, enforcement and taxpayer service, hence reducing transaction costs. It provides a one stop centre for the taxpayers and has resulted in increased tax revenue; increased compliance; reducing objections and tax arrears; response time to taxpayer enquiries; and a improved tax refund system".

Sri Lanka

"Benefits of the LTU include providing better services to taxpayer; higher compliance rate; increase in revenue collection; good work experience for staff; achievement of revenue goals; and prompt collection of tax due".

Singapore

"For Corporate Tax:

There has been substantial value-add from adjustments arising from more focused and thorough reviews

The LTU has been effective in resolving generic issues relating to specific industries

The IRAS has been able to focus our resources on the 5% taxpayers that contributes 75% of the revenue collection

The LTU has allowed for a better understanding of industry specific condition, trends and business practices.

For GST:

We have seen much synergy and focus, thus greater efficiency in the GST administration after the new set-up in 2004. There is more focus and better consolidation and resolution of various issues that are specific to large businesses – technical issues, compliance activities, integration between service and compliance".

New Zealand

"Benefits of the LTU include: Understanding of taxpayers and industry issues; quicker more timely response; earlier identification of issues requiring legislative amendment; focus on risk; and co-ordinated interventions".

IN-DEPTH CASE STUDIES

Pakistan Central Board of Revenue—Large Taxpayer Units

Overview of the Large Taxpayer Units

Under the Pakistan Central Board of Revenue's (CBR) policy of reforms and restructuring over the last several years, CBR has established two regional-based LTUs at Karachi, and Lahore and is currently in the process of forming the third LTU based at Islamabad. The LTUs handle all domestic taxes (income tax, sales tax and central excises), representing a new integrated approach to tax administration, with the broad aims of improving compliance, securing revenue and providing better services to taxpayers. The LTUs serve the largest designated corporate taxpayers, banks, insurance companies and non-resident corporate taxpayers.

Medium Taxpayers Units (MTUs) have also been established at Peshawar, Rawalpindi, Lahore, Quetta and Karachi to extend the model to smaller taxpayers.

The vision and mission of the LTUs are to be "modern, integrated, effective and efficient units of tax administration in Pakistan which promotes mutual trust and satisfaction both for the taxpayers and the tax collectors" and "to provide large taxpayers quality service by helping them understand and meet their tax responsibility by applying tax laws with integrity and fairness to all".

Planning and design phase

Developing the business case

A business case was provided to management and the government for the establishment of three LTUs. The main arguments used in the business case were as follows:

- Need for the integration of data and intelligence across functions and across taxes

- Need for an increase in revenue collected

- Need for a modernisation of taxation infrastructure and remodelling of tax offices – The LTUs (and MTUs) would provide the revenue authority with an opportunity to pilot new approaches to tax administration and assess the nature and magnitude of benefits that could be derived from co-location and the availability of information flows across taxes

- Need for enhancing taxpayer facilitation and reducing compliance cost, starting with large taxpayers, which would enhance tax compliance

- To promote the use of information technology in day-to-day working i.e., give employees access to hardware and software for carrying out day-to-day office work. As well as effectiveness and efficiency improvements, this would also increase data integrity and reduce opportunities for corruption.

Legislative changes required

The units have been established through an administrative order by the competent authority deriving legal authority already available under the relevant statutes namely:

Central Board of Revenue Act, 1924

Income Tax Ordinance, 2001

Sales Tax Act, 1990.

LTU design

Each LTU is based on a functional organisation and is headed by a Director General. All the internal taxes i.e. Income Tax on the one hand and Sales Tax & Federal Excise on the other are co-located and work on functional lines as depicted in Figure 1.

The LTUs also have an open-floor layout with a large reception and facilitation area which allows taxpayers a point of entry to the LTU.

Figure 1. Organisational structure of the LTUs

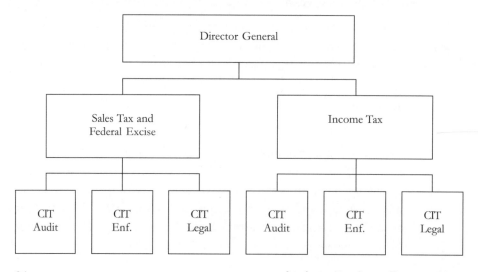

Budgeting

There is an independent Expenditure Wing of the project where officers hired from the Auditor General Department prepare the fiscal monitoring reports, which are submitted to the World Bank and Finance & Planning Division of the Government of Pakistan. All sanctions for spending are approved after rigorous scrutiny, and all expenditure on an annual basis is subject to audit by the Auditor General of Pakistan, as well as the Public Accounts Committee of the Parliament.

Implementation phase

Main milestones

The main phases/milestones coincided with the establishment of modernised units at different stations/locations and these timelines were pre-approved by the government. The first major milestone was a test case or pilot LTU in Karachi in 2002. Implementing computerisation/information technology was a key component in making the unit operational. Thus the LTU had to be equipped with the necessary hardware and software to enable smooth functioning of the unit.

After successful implementation of the test case, a model was developed for subsequent roll-out. CBR established its second LTU in Lahore in 2004 and is currently in the process of rolling out its third LTU.

Throughout the process, stakeholders were consulted via a number of interactive workshops/sessions about the reforms and the LTUs set-up in consequence thereof.

Staffing and training

One of the key objectives of the LTUs was to divert the best available resources to the largest taxpayers – this on one hand facilitates taxpayers in the resolution of their problems and on the other hand allows the handling of complex issues by staff with adequate technical skills.

Staff working in the LTU required professional/technical competence and computer skills. Training provided to the LTU staff focused on the following areas:

Taxation statutes

Analysis of financial statements

Tax audit techniques

Computer skills.

Remuneration and incentives

An incentive-based remuneration system was introduced. Personnel working in the LTUs enjoy a special pay package, which is higher compared with the salaries paid to other government servants at similar scales. The incentive-based remuneration has also helped to foster a new culture within the organisation.

Introduction of technology

Automation has been a key theme behind CBR's policy of administrative reforms. A major IT system, known as the Tax Management System, was introduced in the LTUs, and all the activities of the LTUs are routed through this system. The system has been introduced with the following objectives:

- To create a comprehensive database and record of the functions of the LTUs
- To achieve a paperless environment
- To further strengthen the audit capacity of the unit.

Software has also been introduced to enable large taxpayers to prepare and furnish various statutory source documents, through electronic media.

Implementation challenges

CBR did not face any major challenges/risks during the implementation of the LTU. The fact that the LTU adopted a continuous program of consultation with other business areas was a key factor in overcoming any implementation or coordination issues. It is pertinent to mention that the business areas appreciated the steps taken by the LTU to redress any concerns or grievances.

However, a key risk that was identified was corruption, particularly given the opportunities for closer contact between LTU staff and large taxpayers. In order to eliminate corruption, the LTUs took the following steps.

Any type of liaison with taxpayers or their authorised representatives (e.g. tax consultants) was highly discouraged/disallowed.

An open house/transparent policy was adopted and officers/officials were asked to sit either in the hall or transparent rooms.

Taxpayers'/consultants' visits to the work stations of tax officials/officers was completely disallowed.

Hearing rooms were established and taxpayers/consultants were restricted to that area.

The interface with taxpayers/consultants was restricted to the front office only.

All exemption certificates were issued in 24 hours, and refunds vouchers, orders etc. were sent via courier instead of using personnel from the Tax Department.

The business community has very warmly appreciated the speed of disposal of their grievances, issuance of exemption certificates, receipt of refund vouchers (through mail) without any follow up and minimal inter-action between the tax collector and taxpayer.

Evaluation and review

Success factors

The LTUs have so far proved successful in improving revenue collection, providing a better service to taxpayers and controlling corruption.

The main factors which have contributed to the success of the LTUs include:

- The co-operation of taxpayers
- Acceptance of change by officers and staff of the LTU
- Development of the human resources function
- Better working environment for staff.

Future enhancements

- The Tax Management System needs to be refined so as to cater for the information/work activities which relate to the period prior to the creation of LTUs
- The sales tax and income tax functions for a certain number of cases need to be combined into one office to make the system more efficient. The present system of simple co-location of the two taxes under the same roof instead of a complete merger of income tax and sales tax services/functions is also against the original plan envisaged by The World Bank
- A separate wing needs to be created to conduct industry-based analyses and research to support the audit function
- There is still a need to provide all officers with Internet access and access to subscription services/electronic databases – this requires additional funding
- Funds are required to tempt informers into gathering intelligence and valuable information to support the audit function
- More funding and resources are required to support the audit function e.g. to purchase vehicles, recruit audit support staff, etc.

Advice to others

- The entire workforce needs to be involved in motivational efforts to change the mind-set and culture of the organisation

- The transition phase always needs patience and tactful handling of problems and challenges

- Start with a small number of cases with comprehensive software for automated working

- Any overlapping functions or activities in the LTUs should be looked into and clearly demarcated

- SOPs (standard operating procedures) need to be designed and a constant system of feedback and upgrading the systems should be adopted.

South African Revenue Service—Large Business Centre

Overview of the Large Business Centre

The South African Revenue Service (SARS) Large Business Centre (LBC) was launched in September 2004, in pursuance of a business strategy to increase the compliance levels of this segment while addressing their unique client service needs. The LBC provides a single point of entry for large corporate clients across all tax types and tax administration activities i.e. migration to a one stop shop facility. The aim of the LBC is to enhance the efficiency, certainty and simplicity with which tax matters are resolved, thus facilitating greater compliance.

Situation before implementation

The LBC evolved out of the Corporate Tax Centre (CTC) which was in existence ince 1994. The CTC was staffed with highly skilled SARS auditors and handled approximately 9700 taxpayers. However, the Corporate Tax Centre was limited by a narrow income tax focus and audit engagements being predominantly desk reviews. To this end, it was constrained in not taking a whole enterprise/entity view and in not building a visible field audit presence. Thus, it was decided that an integrated approach to engaging large corporate taxpayers was required to:

- Manage the ever increasing complexity of corporate taxation stemming from increased globalisation of South African companies

- Address the culture of low corporate compliance among South African business, partly flowing from the South African apartheid legacy

- Change the "future rules of the corporate tax game" in terms of matching tax expertise in the private sector and in advancing a collaborative compliance approach

- Move from a reactive to a proactive stance on the dimensions of operations, client engagement and in dealing with emerging risks and trends
- Respond to growing corporate taxpayer needs and expectations
- Build capability to close the large corporate tax gap, in a responsive manner
- Segment the SARS taxpayer market and effectively respond to specific evasion and avoidance trends
- Provide a world class corporate tax service.

Developing the business case

The LBC was established to recognise the unique needs and important contribution (and hence risk) of corporations, large businesses, parastatals (large state owned enterprises) and high net worth individuals to the tax base. SARS wanted to create a specialised unit to look wholistically at the compliance profile of each large client across all tax types, particularly given the ever increasing complex business operations and transactions associated with this segment.

At the same time, SARS wanted to establish a better relationship with large clients, one based on mutual collaboration and consultation, with respect for the tax law. This included providing large taxpayers with greater certainty by offering specialist services and advice from staff who understood their business environment and context in addition to tax legislation. They wanted to move from the former "cat and mouse" or adversarial relationship to one based on mutual respect and co-operation.

Given that large taxpayers had at their disposal significant access to expertise and resources to manipulate their tax affairs to their advantage, SARS also felt that a centralised, "single view of the taxpayer" approach was needed to match this. For example, the use of risk engines that cut across all tax types would be more effective in revealing areas of non-compliance[10] and discerning compliance trends in the large corporate segment.

The envisaged benefits of the LBC included:

- A personalised service offering for taxpayers by servicing all of their tax administration needs and adopting a multi-channel approach with key emphasis on advancing electronic transacting
- Reducing the revenue risk associated with adopting specific tax type audits as opposed to integrated tax audits

---

[10] A customised across-tax-type risk matrix/engine is currently being developed to enhance the risk profiling capability of the LBC.

- Broadening the large corporate tax base especially in respect of non-filing; non-payment and non-disclosure

- Increased voluntary compliance

- Increase in the quantity and quality of audits which includes a migration to focused field audits based on risk and improved understanding of the taxpayer's operations supported by industry knowledge. This signals a shift away from desk reviews that were limited in scope and involved lengthy queries to the taxpayer

- Streamlining the management and processing of taxpayer submissions for improved turnaround, quality and the maintenance of comprehensive and accurate taxpayer information.

Planning and design phase

The first steps

A project team was appointed to drive the design and delivery of the Large Business Centre in accordance with the practices of the Enterprise Project Management Office (EPMO). In designing the LBC, alignment to the SARS mandate and corporate goals was reinforced as well as ensuring overall business alignment thus not creating a stand alone department.

The project included benchmarking visits to Australia, the UK, Sweden and Canada to inform best prevailing practices. These visits revealed that these progressive administrations were turning to specialised centres for large business to deal with the sophisticated and wide ranging tax issues unique to this segment. Three areas of specialisation were also highlighted – tax, industry and relationship management.

In terms of financial resourcing, the LBC was given a zero-base budget with the first full year of operation used to baseline future requirements.

Development of LBC strategic principles

The fundamental principles of the LBC strategy included:

- Comprehensive compliance approach

- One-stop centre

- Ownership of end-to-end processes

- Segmentation of taxpayer base

- Creation of a centre of excellence

- Inclusivity and empowerment.

Development of LBC vision and mission

A vision and mission for the LBC was devised:

"Our vision is to enable and deliver an integrated range of solutions designed to sustain a world class corporate tax and customs system in South Africa. Through this we will:

- Build productive relationships with our stakeholders based on the principles of reliability, mutual trust and respect

- Optimise revenue collection

- Create a tax and customs environment conducive to business growth

- Attract new taxpayers to the South African tax jurisdiction

- Develop a best practice model of corporate tax and customs administration to the benefit of SADC and NEPAD".

"Our mission is to best serve the interests of South Africa and our stakeholders through the optimised collection of all tax and customs revenue from within our identified tax base. We will accomplish this through:

- Professional service delivery

- Firm yet fair enforcement

- The encouragement of compliance

- The application of specialist knowledge, skills and expertise

- Business intelligence and effective risk management".

LBC value proposition

	Through…	Resulting in…
	Developing enhanced relationships with our corporate taxpayers based on intimate knowledge derived from industry sector specialisation	Corporates benefit from a productive interaction that demonstrates insight of their unique business
To promote optimal voluntary compliance at the lowest cost to SARS and the corporate taxpayer	Ensuring a highly effective tax administration offering through professional and competent staff with expert knowledge of all tax types	Corporates benefit through professional, consistent and fair assessment and auditing of their tax obligations and effective dispute resolution when required
	Providing world-class operational excellence with one-stop-single point of entry for all tax types and effective administration	Corporates benefit from cost effective and efficient registration of tax entities, filing of all tax submissions and management of corporate accounts

LBC design and staffing

A decision was made to base the design of the LBC on industry sectors. The current LBC design consists of eight industry sectors in addition to a high net worth individuals sector. The eight sectors include:

- Mining
- Financial services (insurance, banking and diversified financial services)
- Information, communications and technology
- Manufacturing
- Retail trade
- Primary (agriculture, forestry and logging)
- Construction
- General and diverse holdings.

Each sector reports to a sector manager and is staffed with its own risk profiling, assessing, audit and collections teams with an in-depth knowledge of the application of all taxes within their respective industries. Present within each sector is a taxpayer relationship manager who owns client engagement and takes accountability for query resolution.

There is a conscious delineation between the sector manager and relationship manager and the rest of the segment team. This allows compliance staff to be "technical, not tactical" – it is left up to the sector managers and relationship managers to be tactical, hence the necessary business and relationship management skills (discussed further below).

A separate support component within the Large Business Centre provides legal and business intelligence/research services to the segment teams.

Implementation phase

Implementation challenges

The immediate challenge for SARS was to meet the tight project deadlines and the underlying business imperative. On the 1st September 2004, the LBC was officially launched with only 100 staff, no management team and an empty building. On the 3rd September 2004, there was a ministerial release to the public announcing the opening of the Centre! Therefore, it was critical for the LBC to establish itself and build credibility quickly. The upside of this was a greater momentum as well as illuminating critical learning lessons. One particular challenge was the limited ability of the marketplace to provide the crucial skills required by SARS at a reasonable cost of employment.

Operationalisation of the project included the activation of the financial services sector in October 2004 and establishment of regional LBC offices in Western Cape, Eastern Cape and KwaZulu-Natal. The activation of the remaining sectors followed over the next 6-12 months.

Work processes and supporting technology were re-engineered to consolidate all large taxpayers' tax affairs into the LBC over a 12-18 month period. Fortunately, the LBC was able to leverage off existing SARS wide systems and none of the core systems had to be changed. Service levels and best practice benchmarks for standards of operational excellence during the first 12 months were developed as well.

At the same time, the LBC had to create and grow the capability and capacity required to deal with the additional tax types, manage the specific industry sectors and inculcate a customer relationship culture and approach. This included hiring and up-skilling competent professionals including CAs, MBAs, economists and lawyers. A conscious decision was also made to import the top management layer to engender a new culture. For example, sector managers from the private sector with both the necessary tax and industry/business knowledge/experience were sourced. Significant investment was made to secure these external specialist resources, including higher remuneration costs and contract type employment for core competence. At the time of writing, the LBC was aiming to grow its staff complement from its current 348 staff to 600-700.

Securing buy-in and collaboration from other SARS divisions was another key immediate challenge for the LBC as local offices would feel the loss both in meeting revenue targets and in retaining technically competent staff. In hindsight, it would have benefited the transition to engage in further communication, change and internal marketing prior to implementation of the LBC. This would have helped to secure buy-in and support for the LBC.

Evaluation and review

Implementation of the LBC is still in progress. Despite this, the LBC has already proved successful. This is largely due to:

- Full support from the Minister and the Commissioner
- Its management as a separate business unit reporting to the Commissioner via a General Manager who is part of the SARS Executive Committee
- The importation of experienced external management
- A defined budget with some latitude

- A structure based on industry specialisation.

- An operational review was also carried out nine months after inception to evaluate the LBC blueprint, adherence to SARS procedures and to ensure alignment with the overall SARS business plan and model. Key issues that emerged included:

- The need to consolidate the LBC Service Model – Expanding LBC operations in terms of client base, capability and regional presence

- The imperative to sell LBC Value Proposition to taxpayers via business launches, forums, service charter, CEO visits and LBC publications

- The necessity of working towards greater operational efficiency and leverage (via the development of operational plans, information "clean-up", consolidation of some bulk/commodity processes to reduce redundancy, and knowledge and risk profiling/management)

- Increasing collaboration with other business units such as law administration

- Engaging in best practice reviews and ongoing benchmarking against other tax administrations such as the Australian Taxation Office and New Zealand Inland Revenue Department.

- Other more specific focus areas/projects for 2005/2006 include the following:

- Developing a top 200 risk matrix via the newly customised risk engine for better management of this group

- Building capability to address VAT and PAYE administration

- Rolling out the high net worth individuals segment team

- Launching other regional offices

- Defining the taxpayer relationship management role and adopting a consistent service approach guided by toolkit

- Establishing collaborative industry forums

- Developing enhanced knowledge and risk management capacity

- Completing the staff recruitment programme – As mentioned above, the LBC still needs to recruit an additional 250-350 staff. The LBC is also exploring initiatives to assist in retaining and rewarding good staff (e.g. secondments/exchanges to other international tax administrations) as LBC staff are in high demand and vulnerable to being poached by the private sector

- Producing a large business book for taxpayers
- Extending e-filing services for information sharing purposes as well as integrating data links with large business taxpayers.

SARS is also currently looking at extending similar initiatives to cater for the small business market.

Inland Revenue Department of Sri Lanka— Large Taxpayers Unit

Overview of the Large Taxpayers Unit

The Inland Revenue Department of Sri Lanka Large Taxpayers Unit (LTU) was formed under the tax reform program initiated by the IMF in 1995. Given the substantial contribution of large taxpayers to the tax base, it was proposed that a single unit, equipped with the most experienced and qualified staff, would allow large taxpayers to be monitored and supervised more effectively and efficiently.

Headed by a Commissioner, the LTU manages approximately 1000 large taxpayers, accounting for approximately 30% of domestic tax revenue. The main purpose of the LTU is to improve the monitoring and control of large taxpayer's compliance with their basic filing and payment obligations. However, audit and enforcement functions have since been introduced.

Implementation phase

- The most experienced and senior officers were placed in the LTU. However, pay levels and incentive schemes for LTU staff remained the same as for the rest of the Department
- IT systems were introduced for registration, issuing of returns, receiving returns, return data filing, and issuing assessments
- Information gathered by the LTU from large taxpayers was directed to other revenue branches for them to check for additional liability (if any). At the beginning, other revenue branches were not co-operating with the LTU branch, to share information and other necessary materials. However, gradually this obstacle was removed and now the relationship is functioning smoothly
- Resourcing needs and budget were provided though a treasury grant
- Training programmes were provided to LTU staff as an ongoing training scheme within the Department.

Structure of the LTU

Figure 2. Structure of the LTU

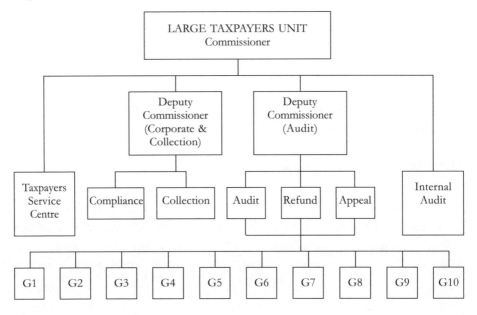

Evaluation and advice to others

- The LTU has been deemed successful. It has improved both compliance monitoring and the way issues are resolved with large taxpayers

- To achieve better output from LTU staff, it is necessary to train them in using IT systems and to leverage off data-links to other public and private enterprises (e.g. Customs Department, Registrar of Motor Vehicles Department and other relevant private enterprises)

- The criteria used to select files is important and revenue authorities need to devote sufficient time and effort to this exercise

- Most importantly, LTU staff need to be well trained to handle LTU files effectively. This branch should be fully computerised with a better information network, linked with the other public and private agencies.

Tanzania Revenue Authority—Large Taxpayers Department

Overview of the Large Taxpayers Department

Tanzania Revenue Authority (TRA) introduced a Directorate of Large Taxpayers on the 1st October 2001, which was subsequently elevated into a full-fledged Large Taxpayers Department (LTD), headed by its own Commissioner, in 2003. This transformation came about as part of wider reform strategies that TRA embarked on with a view to improving, modernising and integrating tax administration in the country.

The LTD now provides a one-stop centre for administering various tax laws including VAT, Income Tax, Excise Duty and Stamp Duty. Its overall goals are to provide better services to large taxpayers, enhance compliance and maximise revenue. It currently handles approximately 300 taxpayers with about 85 employees.

Developing the business case

In line with international best practice, TRA recognised that a differentiated compliance strategy was required to deal with the different segments of the taxpaying community. Given that large taxpayers contributed approximately 70% of domestic revenue in Tanzania, TRA felt it was necessary to establish a dedicated team to monitor the compliance of this segment and to cater to their unique needs.

Drawing on LTU business cases from Kenya, South Africa, Malaysia and Uganda, and advice from IMF and World Bank experts, a business case was presented to the TRA Board of Directors and subsequently approved. The main arguments presented in the business case for establishing the LTD included the following:

- Maximise revenue yield within the legal framework
- Improve audit programs
- Improve collections and management of tax debts
- Provide quality services through a one stop centre for all tax matters
- Pilot new processes, procedures, structures and systems – the LTD was seen as an appropriate pilot centre for testing an integrated approach to tax administration at TRA.

Planning and design phase

The total preparation phase took about nine months. A steering committee was formed to plan the implementation of the LTU. This steering committee undertook the following activities during this planning and design phase:

- Conducted visits to other countries (such as Kenya, Uganda and South Africa) to explore the various options and identify best practices

- Sought advice and supervision from IMF and World Bank experts

- Nutted out the budget required, a site for the LTD, staffing issues, training requirements, criteria to select taxpayers, logistics for transferring and merging taxpayer files, equipment required, computer software and hardware requirements, etc

- Consulted with taxpayers and other external representatives via the Stakeholder's Forum.

The Commissioner General and senior management were also highly involved in the set-up of the LTD, which meant that management commitment was high from the beginning.

LTD design

The current structure of the LTD is functionally-based and organised as follows:

- The LTD is headed by a Commissioner who is appointed by the TRA Board of Directors

- The Commissioner reports to the Commissioner General through the Deputy Commissioner General

- The Commissioner is assisted by a Deputy Commissioner Operations who is also appointed by the Board of Directors

- There are four operational sections namely:

  - Audit – There are four audit groups, each group comprising of two audit teams. Audit cases are allocated to the audit groups based on sectoral specialisation

  - Data Processing and Examination of Returns – The main objective of this section is to ensure availability and sufficient data and establishment of proper declarations of income and tax

  - Debt Management – The main objective of this section is to ensure that the government revenue is collected at the right time, tax defaulters are followed up and appropriate enforcement measures are applied to recover outstanding taxes

  - Technical Services.

  These sections are headed by Managers, each reporting to the Deputy Commissioner Operations, except for the Manager Technical Services who reports directly to the Commissioner

- Other support units which provide support services such as Human Resources, Finance, Legal, Taxpayer Services and Information Systems. The Taxpayer Services unit also provides a front desk service for large taxpayers to make initial contact with the LTD

- Heads of support units report directly to the Commissioner for their day-to-day activities but also report to their respective heads of department within TRA.

The LTD has been granted its own mandate to handle all domestic taxes (apart from customs and international taxes). In line with this modus operandi, operations manuals and guides were reviewed to give power to the unit e.g. VAT and Income Tax manuals.

Audit is the core function of the Department and the main audit objectives are:

- To enhance voluntary compliance and to ensure that taxpayers report accurate income and pay correct amount of tax.

- To educate taxpayers during audits on various tax laws and procedures. Cases for audit are selected based on risk assessment. The section conducts two types of audits, namely:

  (i) Comprehensive audits which are joint audits of all tax liabilities conducted by a team of auditors. The very complex cases which account for about 10% of all cases are audited every year while others are audited at least every three years

  (ii) Issue-oriented audits which are field audits designed to verify specific VAT, PAYE, and Withholding tax issues or errors detected during the processing of monthly returns. Refund audits are also covered under the issue-oriented audit program.

Implementation phase

In October 2001, a Directorate for Large Taxpayers was established under the Commissioner General's Office. This office was relatively small and managed approximately 100 large taxpayers.

Over time, it became apparent that the Large Taxpayers Office was not functioning to its potential. More specifically, the office lacked the independence and power it needed to adequately monitor the compliance of the large taxpayers and provide the level of services that they demanded. It had to compete with other areas on business priorities, funding and on accessing the best qualified staff. Therefore, a decision was made to elevate the Large Taxpayers Office to a Large Taxpayers

Department[11], with its own Commissioner. This meant that it now had its own cost centre, action plans and more freedom to influence HR policy (including the ability to recruit external professionals and industry specialists).

By July 2005, the number of large taxpayers managed by the LTD was 300, contributing about 68% of domestic revenue. Throughout its evolution, the LTD has been careful to ensure that the number of taxpayers it managed was aligned to its capacity.

The criteria for selecting large taxpayers have also changed over time. The initial criteria were:

- Aggregate tax payment exceeding 400 million TSH (approx. 400000 USD) per annum for three consecutive years
- Specific sectors or trade industries such as financial institutions and oil marketing companies.

Later on, the following criterion was added over and above those already in place: Total turnover exceeding 10 billion TSH (approx. 10 million USD).

Staffing and training

There are currently 85 employees working in the LTD. Eighty percent of the staff complement are considered to be in professional roles, with the remaining twenty percent in support roles. Forty two percent of the staff work in the audit section and are assigned to certain sectors or industries.

Most of the staff (except for six auditors who were recruited from the market) were transferred from other revenue departments within TRA. Qualified staff were identified ahead of operationalisation of the LTD which was important as monthly revenue targets had to be met from the word go. The LTD is also currently in the process of recruiting industry specialists from the market e.g. geologists and engineers to better understand business processes.

In terms of the specific skills and expertise required to ensure the effectiveness of the LTD, these included:

- Audit of computerised financial statements
- Tax avoidance practices (especially transfer pricing and thin capitalisation issues)
- Tax evasion techniques
- Systems based audits
- Auditing of mining operations.

---

[11] LTD's experience in operating as a one-stop centre has been taken as a model in the integration of the former Income Tax and VAT Departments to form the Domestic Revenue Department.

Specific training programs (both internal and external) have been provided to LTD staff on the above topics. A broader TRA-wide training program has been implemented to train staff for integrated delivery across the different tax types – this program is known as the 'Total Tax Person' training program.

TRA did not have to introduce different pay levels or incentive schemes to attract and retain staff as the level of compensation across the organisation had been externally benchmarked and was relatively competitive compared to similar organisations.

Legislative changes required

The Tanzania Revenue Authority Act No.11 of 1995 was reviewed to give power to the LTD Commissioner to administer the different revenue laws.

Introducing technology

An integrated tax management system (known as ITAX) and data warehouse is currently being developed and rolled out in TRA and will be used by the LTD[12]. An interbank payment system (known as TISS) has also been introduced to facilitate payments made by large taxpayers to TRA.

Sharing knowledge and intelligence with other areas of TRA

At the moment, the sharing of knowledge and intelligence with other areas of the revenue authority is mostly done on an ad-hoc and manual basis (for example discussions are held to ensure consistency in approaches. The Domestic Revenue Department has also adopted policies and standards that were initially created and tested with the establishment of the LTD so this helps to maintain some consistency). However, once the ITAX system and data warehouse is in place, there will be a corporate repository of client information and history, accessible to all authorised staff.

Implementation challenges

- Meeting customer expectations and providing the level of service they require with limited resources – TRA advises to be careful not to increase the number of large taxpayers managed too quickly. It needs to be in tandem with the capacity of the unit
- Funding limitations
- Meeting training needs and retaining quality staff

---

[12] Those interested in finding out more about ITAX can refer to CATA's publication on 'Implementing computerisation and IT in tax administration', where ITAX has been featured as a case study.

- Modernising processes – making sure technology implementation keeps up
- Meeting and maintaining revenue targets.

Evaluation and review

Success factors

- Support from the IMF/World Bank experts. Development partners also played a key role in performance monitoring
- Exhaustive preparation and planning down to the nitty gritty details – the preparation phase took 9 months
- Conducting visits to other countries and finding out what models they had adopted and the associated pros and cons
- Strict and timely implementation of the action plan
- Dedication and support of the TRA management and the entire staff
- Government support and willingness to pursue the introduction of the LTD
- Co-operation from large taxpayers – many actually want to be part of the LTD
- Ensuring LTD action plans align to corporate plans and objectives
- Establishing the LTD as a separate department with its own Commissioner, rather than establishing it as an office under the Domestic Revenue Department – TRA feels that this is necessary to give sufficient power to the unit.

Future enhancements

TRA still needs to build the capacity of the LTD, adequately train its staff to deal with the ever increasing complexity of the tax affairs of large taxpayers, and introduce initiatives to retain its qualified staff. The LTD has yet to reap the benefits of computerisation as well – it still needs to fully automate its systems, processes and key functions such as assessment, debt management and auditing. This includes integrating forms and templates. A data warehouse is planned for 2007 and this should also help to improve the risk profiling and assessment capability of the LTD. The LTD is planning to roll-out a quality management system (ISO 9001:2000) by June 2006 as well.

TRA have also introduced a 'block management system' (to replace the former physical survey system) to help manage the compliance of SMEs. This system is based on setting up geographical/administrative "blocks" and mandating each block to operate all the key tax administration functions of registering, assessing, collecting and revenue accounting. Given the nature of SMEs in Tanzania, the new block system has the advantage of allowing close physical monitoring and contact with taxpayers.

Uganda Revenue Authority—Large Taxpayers Office

Overview of the Large Taxpayers Office

The Uganda Revenue Authority (URA) relaunched its Large Taxpayers Office (LTO) in February 2005[13], in consultation with the IMF, as part of comprehensive reforms and restructuring of the operations and administration of domestic taxes at URA. The LTO currently handles about 526 large taxpayers across both income tax and VAT and is staffed by 65 employees.

By combining staff resources and talent and equipping staff in these areas with the required specialist skills, the Large Taxpayer Office is able to audit complex operations, provide the taxpayer with accurate and up-to-date information, and create a professional work environment.

Developing the business case

Arguments/reasons for the creation of the LTO included the following:

- To provide sufficient attention to large taxpayers through the creation of a one-stop-centre for the administration of all domestic taxes, and through improved quality and timely services to the segment
- Over 70% of the domestic tax revenue comes from large taxpayers. Therefore it is important to secure revenue and improve management of arrears from this group, through regular audits and immediate collection of tax assessed
- A functional based LTO would enable the operation of domestic taxes in an integrated and better co-ordinated manner
- The LTO can be used as a pilot for testing new processes, procedures, structures and systems which can afterwards be extended to other divisions of the Domestic Taxes Department.

Planning and design phase

The first step undertaken by the URA to assist with the planning and design of the LTO was the establishment of an LTO project team. This team was headed by the

---

[13] URA had previously established a Large Taxpayers Department in 1998. This Department was fully re-designed and this case-study details the implementation of the re-vamped Large Taxpayers Office.

Commissioner Domestic Taxes Department and assisted by the Assistant Commissioner, Large Taxpayer Office, Domestic Taxes Department. The Ministry of Finance, Commissioner General and IMF Tax Advisor were also instrumental in advising and overseeing the implementation of the LTO.

The project team worked on the following issues during the preparatory phase:

- Identifying the basic functions of the LTO (that is, return and payment processing; audits; enforcement of return filing and payment; and taxpayer services)

- Designing the structure of the LTO (see below for more information on the LTO organisational structure)

- Developing the criteria for the selection of taxpayers – This also allowed the URA to predict the number of large taxpayers to be managed, which formed the basis for determining staff and budgeting requirements

- Assessing resource and accommodation requirements including a location for the LTO, office furniture, equipment, computer systems and networks etc

- Determining staffing requirements and selecting/appointing staff

- Establishing a LTO register.

LTO design

The structure of the LTO is one based on both sector specialisation and function as shown in the diagram in Appendix B (page 73). There is also a dedicated taxpayer services front desk to provide large taxpayers with a single point of contact. The LTO is headed by an Assistant Commissioner who reports to the Commissioner Domestic Tax.

Selection criteria

The selection criteria for assigning large taxpayers to the LTO are as follows:

- Turnover above 5 billion UGX (approx. 2.8 million USD)

- Domestic taxes revenue yield above 2 billion UGX (approx. 1.1 million USD)

- Banks

- Holding companies and their associated companies

- Potential revenue yield including all excisable firms.

Implementation phase

After the physical set-up of the LTO (including the transferring of taxpayer files to the LTO), the next phase of implementation consisted of launching the LTO and notifying taxpayers who were transferred to the LTO.

Staffing and training

In terms of staff development, training in the following fields has been deemed necessary:

- Advanced management skills
- Advanced audit techniques
- Computerised accounting packages
- Best practices in collection and enforcement
- Customer care.

No particular incentives or different pay levels apply to staff in the LTO. Remuneration is uniform for similar ranks throughout URA and differences are a result of ranks.

Guidelines have also been introduced to ensure consistency and certainty in how LTO staff interact with large taxpayers. These guidelines include an Audit Manual, Objections Management, and Refunds Procedures.

Introducing technology

URA is currently in the process of developing and rolling out an organisation-wide integrated tax administration system. This system will help to improve the functioning of the LTO.

Sharing information with other areas within URA

Information sharing exists via the URA intranet in which all departments are linked to and through the Data & Information Analysis Division of Domestic Taxes.

In addition, regular meetings with the Customs Department are held to share information.

Implementation challenges

Some of the challenges faced during implementation included:

- Monitoring large taxpayers who were located outside the main city – This has been dealt with by liaising with the smaller offices to monitor the compliance of these taxpayers and ensuring that these offices report to the Assistant Commissioner of the LTO

- Dealing with corruption – Fortunately, the staff restructuring exercise prompted many corrupt staff to leave the organisation.

Evaluation and review

Success factors

- URA's most competent staff were deployed to the LTO under the supervision of a focused management
- Having a clear set criteria for selecting large taxpayers and ensuring that the number of taxpayers managed by the LTO was realistic
- Setting up of the LTO in one building and on one floor made it easy to administer
- The separate taxpayer service counter provided improved customer service for large taxpayers.

Future enhancements

The following changes/refinements still need to occur to make the LTO fully effective:

- Training of staff in specialised areas for continuous improvement
- Automating all processes and integrating URA tax administration
- Implementing a fast track refund processing system for LTO refunds
- Recruiting/accessing trade or industry specialists in particular complex areas like telecommunications, financial institutions
- Allocating taxpayers to particular managers so that all queries from the taxpayers can be directed to the person directly.

UK HM Revenue & Customs—Large Business Service

Overview of the Large Business Service

The previous Inland Revenue's Large Business Office (LBO) and Energy Group (EG) and Customs & Excise's Large Business Group (LBG) are currently in the process of fully integrating to form a single Her Majesty's Revenue & Customs (HMRC) Large Business Service (LBS). Although these areas have had a history of working together (as early as 1994), this complete integration will maximise leverage on their combined knowledge and skills and will allow for a proper assessment of the impact of the actions of large taxpayers, particularly multinational enterprises, on the UK tax base, as well as deliver improvements in effectiveness, efficiency and customer service. The overall aim of the new LBS will be to extend HMRC's knowledge of the relationship with large businesses with an approach based on an expert understanding of tax issues, complemented by a well developed understanding of the commercial and sectoral context in which businesses operate.

Establishment of the LBS is very much work in progress with the final LBS structure to be launched in April 2006. Over the past year or so, HMRC has tested various approaches and consulted with large taxpayers and stakeholders to seek feedback and ideas for developments and refinements. At this stage, what is clear is that the LBS will be established around sectors (rather than regions as in the past), each customer will have a Client Relationship Manager (CRM) and there will be a wholistic picture of risks across all tax types. Customer Relationship Management (CRM) pilots are in progress and five sectors have been established (Financial; Oil and Gas; Industrial and Infrastructure; Consumer Service; and Public Bodies).

The LBS currently employs more than 1900 staff across 84 sites.

A history of joint working

As already mentioned, the two large business areas of the former Inland Revenue and Customs & Excise Departments have had a long history of working together and have piloted various initiatives and projects to develop this partnership. It is worthwhile highlighting some of these initiatives and projects to help stimulate thought amongst revenue authorities who have separate Inland Revenue and Customs departments on how to achieve better integration without embarking on a complete merger. Some of these initiatives and projects include the following:

- The two Departments have piloted a sectoral approach to closer working. Sectors chosen have included Oil, Finance, Food Retail, Motors, Pharmaceuticals, and Telecommunications

- Valuation methodologies used by both Departments in respect of transfer pricing have been examined and feasibility studies undertaken

- Businesses that are common to both areas have had a single point of contact that is available to staff in both Departments via the Intranet site

- Joint IR/C&E teams in a number of large cases were established to determine whether any customer service benefits could be delivered by the two Departments working co-operatively

- Large taxpayers have been kept informed of proposals/initiatives regarding closer working via a Large Corporates Forum (which cuts across tax types) and have provided feedback on these proposals/ initiatives

- Multinational work undertaken by one Department has had input from the other where appropriate

- Sources of knowledge within each department have been identified to determine their usefulness in supporting closer working. This information, together with best practice established from the case pilots and sector pilots, have been pulled together to form a guide to closer working in the large business area. This has been published on the Intranet sites of both departments

- A training program was developed to raise awareness of closer working, providing a better understanding of the revenue regimes and the ways in which information can be exchanged between the Departments

- Closer working has been incorporated into the induction training programs for LBO and LBG

- Legal barriers to closer working have been identified. The two areas have also recognised that the basis of taxation is inevitably different between direct profit-based tax and indirect transaction-based tax and have identified differences and inconsistencies in the treatment of large businesses e.g. the difference in the treatment of small business gifts.

Current issues and challenges

Sectorisation in the LBS

Sectorisation is both the basis of LBS management structure and the tool for organising knowledge of large taxpayers. So far, four sectors have been established (Financial; Oil and Gas; Industrial and Infrastructure; and Consumer Service), but the process is one of ongoing refinement, particularly given that some sectors are obvious/clear-cut whilst others are not, and some groups straddle across sectors (e.g. conglomerates). A Strategic Response Unit will be established to take a cross-sector view, particularly to identify avoidance schemes.

Integration and definition of the customer base

This process has been complicated because essentially it has required the merging of four strands of business, each with a different customer base. Previously, the Inland Revenue's Energy Group looked after the energy sector, but in the last few years, the LBO and EG have worked more closely together in terms of risk assessment. Within the LBO there were two different corporate customer bases, one for the Corporate Tax (CT) arm comprising the 800 highest risk groups and one for the Employer Compliance (EC) arm comprising the 3000 highest risk employers. Both CT and EC operations used a risk assessment process to determine their respective bases and the reason for the differences lies in the different types and levels of risk arising in the employer context on the one hand and the CT context on the other. Customs & Excise's LBG had yet another customer base determined by reference to risk specific to indirect taxes and although there was a core 30% - 40% of common customers there were also some groups that were high risk for direct tax and low risk for indirect tax and vice versa.

Developing the risk management capability

A key challenge for the LBS is to close the tax gap for both direct and indirect taxes. The LBS is developing a single integrated risk management system across all taxes, including a tool kit that will enable Case Teams to look across all taxes to identify where the greatest risks are so that resources can be deployed more effectively. The two main components of the new Risk System are an Entity Risk Score based on the size, complexity, tax governance and behavioural attitude of corporates and a Priority Risk Score for individual risks that provides a 'rating' by which the resource need will be assessed.

Managing the relocation of clients

There were substantial differences in the number of sites occupied by Large Business Teams – around 67 for Customs & Excise and 25 for Inland Revenue. The overall integration of the teams and the move towards sector working has meant that some taxpayers will find themselves dealing with a different office. This relocation needs to be managed.

Finalising the CRM program

At the time of writing, HMRC were still piloting their CRM program. The idea is to have a "Customer Relations Manager" who would:

- Be a single point of contact with responsibility for activity for the customer and for the Department i.e. an account manager role

- Manage the compliance relationship on a continuous basis

- Understand the commercial drivers of the sector generally and for the customer within that sector, including understanding the tax drivers and strategies

- Be accountable for developing and managing the risk assessment

- Be accountable for bidding for resources and ensuring resources are directed in accordance with the risks

- Be able to take an overview of all the taxes and regimes relevant to the business and therefore act as ringmaster calling in assistance as necessary

- Be the first point of contact in the bridge between operations and policy.

A question still to be decided was the extent to which that person would have authority to manage issues, e.g. to have the authority to take a case to the Commissioners and the extent to which authority to negotiate in areas of dispute was associated with that role. One option that had been put forward was to have the ringmaster role pull things together but, when technical issues were to be discussed, to talk directly to the person with responsibility for the policy or technical issues around that. Another possibility was to have two people, one as the point of contact/front person/account manager but a second person as the team negotiation and settlement specialist around technical issues. It was not yet clear whether or not this needed to be the same person.

Key integration lessons so far

- The business must own the program objectives and vision
- The Program Team in charge of planning and implementing the integration must be fully aware of current operational activity
- Operational people should design and own the products of the projects
- A collaborative approach is essential, involving all stakeholders
- Good communications and the flexibility to respond to change should be built into the program
- At the head of the program team should be people who together understand all aspects of the business.

Zambia Revenue Authority—Managing the Compliance of Large Traders

Overview of the arrangement in ZRA

Zambia Revenue Authority (ZRA) does not have a single large taxpayers unit or department in the traditional sense of the term. However, it has established dedicated teams to manage the compliance of large or complex traders. In fact, there are two dedicated teams – one for managing VAT compliance and one for managing direct taxes, and each team has relative autonomy to set its own budgets, work plans and targets. Since the establishment of ZRA in 1994, ZRA has made a conscious decision to develop the two capabilities separately to cultivate specialisation and expertise in the tax types in a short amount of time. The two teams have also had more of a compliance focus rather than service focus, so it has made sense to operate as such.

However, whilst the two large trader teams work separately, the two teams do exchange information (e.g. financial statements and emerging issues/risks) and try to coordinate the timing of requests and audits wherever practical. Information is also shared with the Customs Department as required. In addition, corporate functions and systems exist to facilitate an integrated approach to tax administration at ZRA. For example, there is corporate database and IT system (known as ITAS) accessible to all inspectors that allows for intelligence and taxpayer data to be shared efficiently and effectively between the VAT and Income Tax Departments, as well as the Customs & Excise Departments. There is also a corporate Taxpayers Advice Centre and Investigations Unit that cuts across all tax types.

Direct Taxes Large Traders Team

The Direct Taxes Large Traders Team (known as Lusaka C) was established under the Direct Tax Modernisation Program, a component of the Department of International Development (DFID) funded Zambia Revenue Authority Consolidation Project, to manage the complexity and risk posed by multinationals and large traders. Other teams – Lusaka A and Lusaka B were established to monitor the compliance of small/medium companies and individuals/self employed respectively.

Team Structure

Currently, the Direct Taxes Large Traders Team is headed by an Assistant Commissioner who reports to the Commissioner of Direct Taxes. Under the Assistant Commissioner is a team of four senior inspectors and four inspectors. Each inspector is assigned to a particular industry sector – Banking and Finance; Mining; Manufacturing and Construction.

Selection criteria

The criteria used to select a large trader includes those with a turnover greater than 5 million, multinationals, or those in one of the particular industry sectors listed above or presents sufficient complexity or risk in tax affairs.

Training

In developing the capacity of the team, inspectors in the Large Traders Team attended in-house training programs provided by international experts and consultants in areas such as transfer pricing, audit of multinationals and banking and insurance. Staff also attended external courses such as those run by CATA.

In order for inspectors to do their work effectively and efficiently, it was considered really important for inspectors to gain access to relevance reference material and handbooks such as taxation periodicals, domestic and international tax statutes, and trade and professional publications. Some of the specific publications recommended by DFID at the time of their review included:

- OECD Transfer Pricing Guidelines and Model Double Tax Convention
- Various publications from the International Bureau of Fiscal Documentation Catalogue
- Dun &Bradstreet's "Who Owns Whom" publication (which allows users to understand the group of companies of which the company or companies under consideration form part).

Remuneration and incentives

For both the Direct and Indirect Large Traders Teams, pay and incentives are commensurate with the rest of the organisation. However, benchmarking is done with comparative institutions such as banks to ensure that salaries are competitive. A new performance management system is also being introduced which will act to better reward performance.

Indirect Taxes Large Traders Team

The Indirect Taxes Large Traders Team was formed at the time ZRA was established as an autonomous revenue authority. It currently manages approximately 100 taxpayers with 12 staff (qualified accountants and economists).

Team Structure

The Team is headed by a Senior Inspector who reports to an Assistant Commissioner who in turn reports to a Deputy Commissioner (as shown in Figure 3 below).

Selection criteria

The selection of large traders is flexible and is based on tax throughput greater or equal to 3 billion ZMK, suppliers involved in handling complex tax areas including branch networks, complex computerised accounting systems, trader tax compliance history, accounting document throughput, liability problems and group co-ordination requirements and responsibilities.

The above parameters are used with guidance of local knowledge, availability of resources, and profiled risk treatments as determined at both Divisional and Corporate levels.

Each year, a business case for why a trader is selected and monitored is provided and approved by management. All contacts with large traders are also planned at

Figure 3. Structure of VAT Large Traders Team

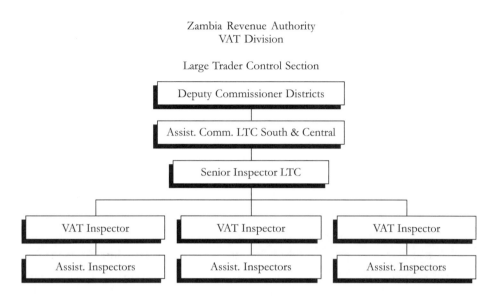

Zambia Revenue Authority
VAT Division

Large Trader Control Section

Deputy Commissioner Districts

Assist. Comm. LTC South & Central

Senior Inspector LTC

| VAT Inspector | VAT Inspector | VAT Inspector |
| Assist. Inspectors | Assist. Inspectors | Assist. Inspectors |

the beginning of the year and all appointments are approved by the leader of the Team.

Training

Inspectors were trained in investigation and audit skills. In comparison to direct taxes, the VAT legislation is relatively simpler and hence inspectors required less specific training.

Key challenges

- Establishing the physical office – Considerable thought had to be invested into finding the office space and equipping it with the required equipment and resources

- Staff selection, training and retention – Finding, training and retaining qualified staff has been an ongoing challenge. The work to be undertaken requires specialist knowledge of the tax laws, high level auditing and investigating skills and/or understanding of industry and business. Working in the area also allows inspectors to acquire high level skills which are highly sought after in the private sector. As such, there is a constant need for more manpower in the Teams.

- Continuous training of staff – Ongoing training is required to keep pace with developments in the environment. Currently there are many complex issues around partnerships and the retail and wholesale sector is becoming a new high risk area. The Teams are trying to skill inspectors to have a more wholistic understanding of business processes to help them identify risks. The constant change in the environment has meant that the industry sectors monitored by the Teams may change over time.

- During the review conducted by DFID, it was found that the tax legislation needed considerable overhauling. It was a challenge to concurrently establish the Direct Taxes Team and review the legalisation at the same time. With the aid of Crown Agents, new provisions to deal with transfer pricing and thin capitalisation were introduced. This resulted in new cases to investigate but care was taken not to overburden the inspectors by taking on more cases that they could handle.

- Fine-tuning case selection – Ongoing work needs to be done to fine-tune how cases are currently selected for review by the Direct Taxes Team. At the moment the system may pick up for example very small miners and the Team cannot investigate these cases with its limited resources. There needs to be refining of the criteria used to select cases.

Possible future enhancements

Although the current structure of small and specialised teams to manage the compliance of large traders in both direct and indirect taxes has suited ZRA's needs to date, in the future, ZRA may look to integrating the teams or at least have inspectors working much closer together. In addition, the effectiveness of the Teams will improve once the new ITAS system has bedded in and the audit modules refined to evaluate risk across tax types.

COMMON THEMES AND GOOD PRACTICES

Whilst the concept of an LTU has been around since the 1980s, ever since the IMF recommended their establishment, research conducted for this publication suggests that they have since evolved from the traditional compliance-focused arrangement. Member countries that have recently established an LTU in the past year or so, or have revamped/restructured their existing LTU, all have the following common characteristics or goals in mind:

- They seek to achieve an integrated approach to tax administration (including risk management), cutting across all tax types (and ideally including customs and excise), with end-to-end ownership of operations and functions impacting on large taxpayers

- They aim to provide a one-stop-shop to large taxpayers, espousing a customer service culture and pursuing a co-operative compliance approach to help reduce compliance burden and promote the proactive management of issues and risks

- They are staffed with the most competent and qualified auditors, lawyers, researchers, industry specialists and customer relationship managers to match the demands of large taxpayers and the resources and expertise available to them

- Sectorisation is a common basis for organising the LTU, permitting a better understanding of business practices, environmental/economic impacts and risks to revenue. Even LTUs that are organised along functional lines have some degree of industry/sector specialisation incorporated into the LTU design

- The introduction of IT systems has played a critical role in making this new mode of integrated working possible

- Consultation with staff, large taxpayers and other stakeholders (such as tax professionals) during the design and piloting of initiatives plays an important part in securing buy-in and support for the LTU.

- Below, we elaborate on the common themes, lessons and good practices arising from the case studies and the existing literature.

Consider sector specialisation as the basis for structure of the LTU

As mentioned earlier, and indeed recommended by the IMF, it is becoming increasingly common for revenue authorities to base the organisation of their LTU on certain industries or sectors. Even for LTUs that are not primarily organised by industry or sector, there is usually still some degree of industry specialisation, for example for compliance resources (i.e. active compliance and interpretation). At the most basic level, revenue authorities should at least have officers or access to individuals who have specialist industry knowledge.

Sectorisation has the benefits of allowing revenue staff to develop an in-depth understanding of the legislative requirements, common business practices and revenue risks in the chosen sectors. At the same time, large taxpayers get to deal with competent staff who understand their business and tax issues, thus reducing the compliance burden and hopefully improving tax compliance. According to a review done by the UK Inland Revenue[14], large taxpayers commented that their experience of the Inland Revenue was best where the Department had established a special focus on particular sectors. For example, there were positive comments about the Oil Taxation Office, where the Inland Revenue has long had a specialist team, and the ability of companies to have real time discussion about the tax treatment of complex commercial transactions, point to the quality of service that can accompany specialisation.

Although sectorisation sounds like a good idea in principle, implementing it in practice can be a bit more difficult. Whilst some sectors are fairly obvious (such as 'mining/oil' and 'banking and finance'), other sectors are not so easy to define (for example 'chemicals' can include bulk chemicals to small scale production of complex chemicals, some of which are drugs or even food ingredients). Some large taxpayers (e.g. conglomerates) also cut across sectors. Therefore, it is pertinent that the LTU thinks carefully about how large taxpayers will be classified and managed.

To help choose and define a sector, a revenue authority can look at:

- Major sectors of the economy
- Complexities of particular industries or businesses
- Special tax rules and regulations
- Common tax risks
- Need for consistency[15].

---

[14] UK Inland Revenue (2001). 'Review of links with business'. Available at: http://www.hmrc.gov.uk/pbr2001/businesslinks.pdf.

[15] Advice provided to 2005 CATA CTIC and AMP course participants by HMRC.

As well as or instead of sectorisation, another way of organising the LTU is on areas of high risk e.g. mergers, acquisitions and capital gains.

Finally, whilst this publication advocates sectorisation and specialisation, there still needs to be effective sharing of information between areas/groups within the LTU. This helps to ensure consistency and coordination of actions and communications. There is an equally pressing need for coordination, consistency and communication across the LTU/non-LTU divide.

Consider establishing client relationship managers

If providing a one-stop-shop to facilitate large taxpayers is one of the key objectives of the LTU, revenue authorities should consider establishing client relationship managers to provide large taxpayers with a single point of entry/contact into the LTU. The LTUs of the UK, South Africa and Australia (amongst others) have all adopted this concept. If this option is not practical or feasible, then there should at least be a dedicated taxpayer services area (ideally within the LTU) where taxpayers can gain access to the LTU, as in the case of Pakistan, Sri Lanka, Tanzania and Uganda. Having a separate taxpayer services area also has the added benefit of minimising the contact audit and technical staff can have with large taxpayers, thus reducing opportunities for corruption (further discussion on controlling corruption can be found below).

There is no single best solution as to the exact roles and authority a client relationship manager should perform and possess and revenue authorities need to devote sufficient time to working through these issues. In the Australian Taxation Office (ATO), the client relationship manager is the main interface between the ATO and the large taxpayer, and has responsibility for proactively coordinating two-way communications and knowledge flows. ATO client relationship managers build client relationships by having regular contact with the client – this creates an opportunity to ensure the client is aware of ATO initiatives or services such as new electronic channels for providing information or information on the ATO Compliance Program. Client relationship managers also perform a valuable role in ensuring the client is meeting obligations such as payments and lodgments and where significant deviations in payment patterns occur, seek feedback from clients. Other duties include:

- Liaising with other areas within the ATO to share client issues and market intelligence
- Collecting feedback from the client on ATO issued and industry specific documentation

- Assisting in the distribution and collection of surveys and questionnaires to selected key clients for revenue forecasting purposes.

In the UK, the client relationship manager has traditionally acted as a "ring master" and, in the LBO at least, chief negotiator with a powerful voice in determining the conduct of a case, where appropriate through Commissioners proceedings and beyond. It remains to be seen whether client relationship managers in the new Large Business Service will have the authority to take a case to the Commissioner and negotiate in areas of dispute.

The LTU should administer all tax types

By having the LTU responsible for administering all tax types, the LTU is better positioned to look wholistically at a business and identify, assess and mitigate risks. It also helps to reduce the compliance burden on large taxpayers by reducing the number of interactions and interventions required, for instance, reducing the need for separate audits or requests for information issued from the VAT, income tax and customs departments.

Whilst the LTUs of a number of revenue authorities administer all tax types by having complete ownership of end-to-end operations and functions impacting on large taxpayers (including registration, processing, collections and enforcement, audit, taxpayer services, litigation etc) other LTUs delegate certain functions to corporate areas (e.g. registrations and processing), keeping mostly higher level functions in the LTU (such as audit, risk assessment, and provision of advice). If the latter model is to be adopted, the LTU needs to at least have access to a centralised IT system[16] or database, so that information can be shared and a single, across tax type view of a taxpayer, and their accounts and history of interactions can be obtained to help facilitate an integrated approach to tax administration.

Ensure the LTU has sufficient power and autonomy

To be fully effective, the LTU should be headed by a senior manager (ideally directly accountable to the head of the tax administration) and have sufficient autonomy and power to manage its own budget, conduct planning activities, determine operational policies, and identify and meet resourcing requirements. Without sufficient power and autonomy, the LTU may find itself competing with

---

[16] Readers interested in implementing IT may wish to refer to CATA's publication on 'Implementing computerisation and IT for tax administration', available from CATA's website: www.cata-tax.org.

other areas on business priorities and resources, and may be limited by corporate policies and procedures not suited to the dynamic nature of the relationship with large taxpayers.

However, at the same time, it is critical that other key client segments are not ignored as this could build resentment both internally (e.g. business areas feeling like they do not have access to the same tools and resources as the LTU) and externally (e.g. large taxpayers may feel they are bearing too much of the tax burden or small taxpayers feel as if the 'big end of town' get special treatment from the revenue authority). An unbalanced approach can take a tax administration into the political arena with allegations of the government of the day "cosying up" to big business. As pointed out by the IMF, the revenue authority needs to apply any lessons learned from the LTU and extend modernisation efforts achieved in LTUs to the rest of the organisation.

Review capabilities and capacity before operationalising

From the case studies conducted, members commented on the value of reviewing the capabilities and capacity of the organisation *before* the actual operationalisation of the LTU. This way, the LTU can "hit the ground running" so to speak and achieve collection targets (or other key performance indicators) and build credibility from the launch date. This process of review includes:

- Identifying suitably qualified and competent staff (including managers) that could be transferred to the LTU and training/skilling them up to the task

- Putting in place bespoke, advanced training and development programmes to equip LTU officers with the specialist knowledge and skills needed to handle big business and the complex challenges it generates

- Developing and embarking on a recruitment program to meet the necessary resourcing requirements of the LTU (see below for a discussion of the skill sets required)

- Estimating how many large taxpayers would need to be managed (based on the selection criteria) and matching resourcing requirements to this.

Devote sufficient time to the planning and design phase

As well as reviewing capabilities and capacity, enough time needs to be devoted to the planning and design phase to ensure a smooth implementation process (for example, TRA dedicated 9 months to the task!). During this phase, the revenue authority should consider the following activities:

- Establishing a dedicated project team (with direct access to the head of the tax administration) to embark on the planning and design process

- Visiting other agencies to identify lessons and best practices

- Designing and deciding on the structure and functions of the LTU

- Working out the accommodation and equipment requirements, including software and hardware, Internet access, subscriptions to relevant periodicals and publications etc

- Planning the actual logistics e.g. when staff will be moved, how long it will take to consolidate files etc

- Developing/re-engineering work processes and tool kits

- Setting key performance indicators for monitoring and evaluating the success of the LTU

- Consulting with relevant internal and external stakeholders.

Skills set required in the LTU

To match the resources and expertise available to large taxpayers and meet their demands, LTU staff need to be adequately equipped with the skills and competencies to deal with the complex affairs of large taxpayers. Table 2 below summarises the high level skill sets required in the LTU. These skill sets do not represent the competencies required in an individual, but the LTU as a whole. Nor does it imply that these skill sets are mutually exclusive – for example, industry knowledge is useful for staff working in either active compliance, customer relationship or interpretation.

Consider enhanced remuneration and career prospects for LTU staff

LTUs have an extremely difficult time in finding and retaining skilled and experienced staff, including accounting, technical and IT specialists. This is because such staff are highly sought after, particularly in the private sector where salaries and career prospects are typically better than in the public service.

Revenue authorities should attempt to provide salaries that are comparable to or better than similar institutions not only to attract and retain staff but to help lessen

Table 2. High level skill sets required in the LTU[17]

Active Compliance	Client Relationship Management	Industry Knowledge	Interpretation
Auditing skills Investigation and analytical skills In-depth knowledge of tax avoidance practices, transfer pricing, thin capitalisation, international tax issues etc Project management skills IT skills e.g. for computer assisted verification Forensic accounting	Relationship management/ interpersonal skills Professional attitude Ability to understand the issue (not limited to technical discussions) Knowledge of the relevant internal contacts that may apply to the taxpayer Deep understanding of the issues faced by participants in an industry and the inner operations of the industry Negotiation skills	Deep understanding of the issues and business reality faced by participants in an industry and the inner operations of the industry Technical knowledge of the implications of transactions carried out by the industry Relationship management skills Negotiation skills Application of technical decisions/ responses so that they are actually workable in practice	Legal research skills Technical skills to support interpretation, setting of precedents and policy development

corrupt practices[18]. At the very least, revenue authorities should conduct regular benchmarking of pay against comparable organisations to ensure they are offering competitive salaries and/or intangible and tangible benefits. Revenue authorities should also consider assigning certain LTU staff to a higher pay classification to match the higher level of qualifications, knowledge and experience required for the job.

Some countries have de-linked salaries of revenue administration staff from the general public service, thus giving management the freedom to pay market salaries. This also allows more freedom in dismissing poor performing staff. Other countries (such as South Africa) have gone one step further and have introduced 2-5 year contract arrangements which specify performance requirements, in return for higher pay and benefits.

---

[17] Adapted from: Deloitte (2005). 'Final report: Review of the GST large corporate compliance program' (prepared for the Australian Taxation Office). Available at: http://ato.gov.au/content/downloads/GSTLCCPFinalReport.pdf.

[18] Higher pay on its own does not prevent corruption. It needs to be coupled with strong internal control mechanisms and effective sanctions that make it easier to dismiss staff. See Fjeldstad, O., Kolstad, I. & Lange, S. (2003). 'Autonomy, incentives and patronage: A study of corruption in the Tanzania and Uganda Revenue Authorities', Chr. Michelsen Institute (available at: http://www.cmi.no/pdf/?file=/publications/2003/rep/r2003-9.pdf).

Obviously, pay and related monetary benefits are not the only factor in attracting, retaining and motivating staff to perform. Revenue authorities need to review their HR strategies to:

- Provide staff with ongoing learning and development opportunities (this may include for example promotion based on merit rather than seniority and exchange programs with other revenue authorities)

- Reward and recognise high performers

- Allow jobs to be designed (wherever possible) to empower[19] and engage staff

- Introduce performance management systems to monitor and manage performance

- Provide non momentary benefits such as retirement benefits, annual leave and physical working conditions.

Introduce mechanisms to control corruption

Unfortunately, the mere fact that LTUs allow a closer working relationship with large taxpayers, also translates into increased opportunities for corrupt activities, without adequate control mechanisms in place. Revenue authorities can help control corruption in the LTU by:

- Standardising procedures – By designing and communicating clear and consistent frameworks, procedures and rules, this helps to increase transparency, reduce discretion of officials and strengthen accountability and possibilities for controls. Standardised procedures should also limit one-on-one contacts between officials and taxpayers and reduce the number of forms/approvals needed (for example through the introduction of "one-stop procedures"). Although the client relationship manager concept referred to earlier seems to go against this argument, revenue authorities can clearly delineate the responsibilities and authority of this role to prevent abuse of the position. For example, at SARS, the relationship manager does not make technical decisions. Similarly, many LTUs have a separate taxpayer service area so that auditors do not have unnecessary contact with large taxpayers

---

[19] Although this does not mean providing all staff with discretion over important decisions, such as those related to the determination of tax liabilities, selection of audits, litigation, etc. Empowerment is about the ability of staff to influence and provide feedback on what they do on a day-to-day basis.

- Introducing integrity systems – LTU services should be subject to regular internal and external controls. In order to make controls effective, performance standards (relating to revenue targets and service standards) as well as codes of conduct, providing for principles such as conflict of interest, confidentiality of information etc., should be in place. These codes need to be backed up by effective sanctions, which should include internal disciplinary measures for minor offence and the involvement of law enforcement agencies for more serious cases of fraud and corruption. The establishment of special vigilance units can support internal controls. Taxpayer surveys are useful tools to diagnose problems and monitor the ongoing effects of reforms. A credible, independent and accessible appeals mechanism should be available to taxpayers[20].

Manage the transfer of taxpayers to the LTU

Managing the transfer process of large taxpayers to the LTU tends to be overlooked, but is an important phase nonetheless. Particularly for revenue authorities without existing centralised IT systems and databases, the transfer and consolidation of hardcopy taxpayer files can take a long time and prevent the LTU from achieving an integrated approach to tax administration. A decision also needs to be made on whether all present litigation or ongoing proceedings and pending matters get transferred to the LTU.

A number of revenue authorities also commented on the difficulties encountered in obtaining large taxpayer files from business areas that were reluctant to give them up! This was usually due to the fact that they still had revenue targets to meet and that losing the files of certain large taxpayers would impact significantly on their performance. Therefore, it is important for the revenue authority to revisit and revise performance indicators to prevent this scenario from occurring.

Revenue authorities need to consider any impacts on large taxpayers as well. For example, if large taxpayers are used to dealing with a particular office, they will need to be informed of any changes in arrangements.

Manage expectations, internally and externally

As part of any change process, the expectations of internal and external audiences needs to be managed by communicating openly, frequently, and consistently the

---

[20] Adapted from the U4 Utstein Anti-Corruption Resource Centre (see http://www.u4.no/helpdesk/helpdesk/queries/query13.cfm).

aims, goals, value proposition, scope, process/milestones, progress, impacts and limitations of the change initiative. This could be done via meetings, workshops, consultative forums, paper products (e.g. newsletters, brochures), mass media (e.g. newspapers, television) and electronic media (e.g. Intranet, Internet).

In establishing a LTU, it is important to manage the expectations and communicate effectively with internal audiences (i.e. LTU staff, senior management, other business areas, etc.) because it helps to secure support and co-operation for the LTU (especially in the transfer of files to the LTU!) and allay any fears or misconceptions. In support of this observation, Pakistan's Central Board of Revenue commented in their case study that a continuous program of consultation with other business areas was a key factor in overcoming any implementation or coordination issues.

Externally, communicating with large taxpayers, tax advisors and other intermediaries, and the media, helps to establish buy-in and build credibility of the LTU. If done properly it also sends out a message to the wider community that the LTU has the knowledge, skills and business intelligence to detect and counter tax evasion and avoidance.

However, it is important to keep in mind that the act of managing expectations entails being realistic and outlining any limitations. There is no point in raving on about the excellent and comprehensive service a large taxpayer will receive if the LTU is only currently equipped to deal with a limited number of large taxpayers and cannot extend its services to all large taxpayers.

CO-OPERATIVE COMPLIANCE – A MORE RECENT DEVELOPMENT IN THE MANAGEMENT OF LARGE TAXPAYERS

As mentioned in the introduction to this publication, several countries have moved towards adopting a co-operative compliance approach in dealing with large taxpayers. This approach was pioneered by the Australian Taxation Office and as put forth by the South African Revenue Service, a co-operative compliance approach seeks to "change the rules of the corporate tax game", moving from a traditionally adversarial and authoritarian relationship to a new one based on mutual respect and understanding.

Co-operative compliance encompasses:

- Recognition that large taxpayers are major contributors to revenue, the economic performance of a country and the overall management of the tax system and that both large taxpayers and the revenue authority have mutual obligations to ensure the integrity and legitimacy of the tax system in the eyes of the wider community

- Building open, transparent and co-operative relationships with large business – Compliance strategies that are understood by business and which take into account the real world concerns of business will encourage voluntary compliance. Greater co-operation will also help to identify weaknesses in the law and difficulties in its administration and identify solutions and ways to improve it. Finally, an improved mutual understanding will assist in the identification of win-win practices and approaches.

In practice, co-operative compliance may include the following initiatives:

- Providing advance rulings on tax (and perhaps customs) issues to provide more certainty and consistency to large taxpayers contemplating significant new transactions

- Providing decisions on the tax effects of completed transactions of significance nearer to real time

- Enlisting the corporate's co-operation in the risk assessment process in return for earlier determination of liabilities

- Developing advance pricing agreements, again to provide for more certainty and consistency in cross border transactions between related parties

- Developing clear audit protocols and communicating these to large taxpayers – this aims to increase transparency and helps to reduce the compliance burden

- Establishing consultative forums so that large taxpayers (and their advisors) can get involved in providing ideas and feedback for operational policy and overcoming difficulties in the tax code[21]

- Actively educating/encouraging large taxpayers to recognise tax risks as part of good corporate governance[22] – Regulatory and tax compliance has become an increasingly important focus for business. The passage of the Sarbanes-Oxley Act 2002 in the US, as well as legislation and practice with similar objectives in a number of other countries have resulted in a heightened awareness of effective tax risk management as an important aspect of good corporate governance

- Introducing 'frameworks of compliance' where large taxpayers agree to observe defined standards of compliance in return for higher levels of service and support and less intrusive interventions with the associated lower compliance costs[23]

- Conducting exchange programs for LTU staff and tax specialists located within the tax departments of large businesses. Although, the author

---

[21] As well as consultative forums, the Australian Taxation Office (ATO) is planning to convene a large market symposium in April/May 2006. As well as launching its 'Large Business and Tax Compliance' booklet, this symposium will cover topics such as ATO directions and performance, commercial and business directions, developments in tax law, compliance processes and services and key risks and common adjustment areas. In addition, the ATO is planning to invite corporate group executives to meet with senior tax officers on a half yearly basis to discuss progress of any compliance activity and significant events in the corporate's business or revenue performance.

[22] See for example: http://www.ato.gov.au/corporate/content.asp?doc=/content/sp200303.htm.

[23] The US Internal Revenue Service is conducting a pilot program, the Compliance Assurance Process (CAP), for large business taxpayers. Under this pilot program, the IRS's Large and Mid-size Business Division is working with large business taxpayers to identify and resolve issues prior to the filing of a tax return. The objective of the program is to reduce taxpayer burden and uncertainty while assuring the IRS of the accuracy of tax returns prior to filing, thereby reducing or eliminating the need for post-filing examinations. The CAP will reduce taxpayer burden through the contemporaneous exchange of information about completed events and transactions that affect tax liability, rather than through the traditional examination process. The CAP will also foster compliance by helping the IRS achieve its goal of shortening examination cycles and increasing currency for taxpayers while enhancing the accurate, efficient, and timely final resolution of increasingly complex corporate tax issues. In addition, the program will assist in increasing audit coverage by providing a more efficient use of audit resources. Finally, the program will allow taxpayers to better manage tax reserves and ensure more precise reporting of earnings on financial statements.

was not aware of any revenue authority that had embarked on such a program, it is a potential initiative and represents the highest test of transparency as it allows both parties to develop and in-depth understanding of internal processes/procedures and issues.

But whilst adopting a co-operative compliance approach is mostly achievable and constructive, it can be difficult to apply in practice. Often, there is a delicate balance between achieving consistency and being responsive. For example, the ATO has been criticised by large taxpayers in terms of its timeliness in providing private binding rulings and unwillingness to provide advance, informal advice. But if the ATO allowed early informal discussion of issues, will this compromise consistency in approach? Revenue authorities also need to be careful that it is not viewed by the wider community as providing large taxpayers with special treatment. In addition, the prevailing tax culture would be a significant factor for revenue authorities to consider, particularly those in developing countries, before adopting a co-operative compliance approach.

Appendix A

List of member countries that participated in the quantitative survey

Australia

Barbados

Botswana

Cameroon

Kenya

Malaysia

Malta

New Zealand

Nigeria

Pakistan

Papua New Guinea

Singapore

South Africa

Sri Lanka

St Kitts & Nevis

St Lucia

United Republic of Tanzania

Trinidad & Tobago

Appendix B

Uganda Revenue Authority. The structure of the Large Taxpayer Office (refers to page 46).

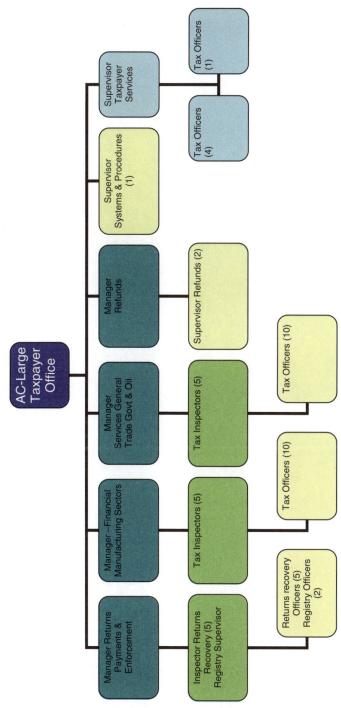